GW01466442

GENERAL GORDON ON GOLGOTHA

LETTERS TO THE ROYAL HOUSEHOLD
FROM JERUSALEM IN 1883.

GENERAL CHARLES GORDON OF KHARTOUM

TO SIR JOHN COWELL,
COMPTROLLER TO THE HOUSEHOLD OF
QUEEN VICTORIA

EDITED BY
ROSALIND MERYON

General Charles Gordon, 'Chinese Gordon', formerly the Governor General of Sudan, military engineer and tactician, Biblical scholar – the archetypal Victorian hero, spent a year in Palestine in 1883. He sent letters with his thoughts and theories concerning the Biblical sites to the Household of Queen Victoria, where his friend, another soldier, Sir John Cowell, was Comptroller. This collection has previously never been published and is owned by The Garden Tomb, Jerusalem which General Gordon considered a probable site of the Resurrection of Jesus Christ. The adjoining hillside, called Skull Hill, or Golgotha, with its image of a giant skull in the rock face, he surmised had to be the Place of the Crucifixion. When Gordon was tragically killed in Khartoum within a year of leaving Jerusalem, after a prolonged siege of that city, his name became a British legend. It was as a result of a public subscription that the Garden Tomb was later purchased. Over a quarter of a million visitors now visit The Garden Tomb each year, view "Skull Hill" (Gordon's Golgotha) and make their own decisions about the event that changed the world 2000 years ago. Seeing the City through Gordon's writing, his illustrations and the photographs is a step back in time to a place where little development had taken place since the days of the Roman Empire. There is also valuable source material for the historian and Biblical geographer.

First published 2012 PUBLISHED BY

THE GARDEN TOMB,

P.O. BOX 19462

JERUSALEM 91193

ISBN 978-1-904459-51-4

Printed in Jerusalem

«Habesch» The Commercial Press

Copyright

All rights reserved. No part of this publication may be reproduced, stored in or introduced into a retrieval system, or transmitted, in any form or by any means (electronic, mechanical, photocopying, recording or otherwise), without the prior written permission of the publisher of this book.

EDITOR'S NOTE

The compilation of the letters written by General Charles George Gordon from Jerusalem in 1883 has been a great privilege for me. This man, "martyr and misfit", as one of his biographers titled their work, was a man who will always be associated with the Garden Tomb, convinced as he was by its authentic location, where we now live and work. Although already famous before his visit to Jerusalem for his military achievements, he became a legendary figure after his tragic death in Khartoum only a year later.

I have long been interested in General Gordon. One of a line of British military officers in my family and living in Jordan as a young child, my father was Commander of the Arab Legion Artillery, gave me a special love for the Holy Land. We would travel to East Jerusalem, then a part of Jordan, where my mother visited Bertha Vester at the American Colony, her daughter Anna-Grace, was also a family friend of ours. Bertha, daughter of Horatio and Bertha Spafford, founders of the American Colony, had witnessed many tumultuous events in this city during her lifetime. She entertained General Allenby, Colonel T E Lawrence, and the other British commanders of the early twentieth century. However, one man she remembered, as a five year old child, was General Charles Gordon, 'the fabulous hero of Sudan', as she refers to him in her book, 'Our Jerusalem'. Bertha says that he lived in a rented house in Ein Kerem, a village west of Jerusalem. He would ride out on a white donkey to visit her parents at the large house they lived high on the wall of the Old City, reached from steps beside the Damascus Gate. "Whenever General Gordon came to our house, a chair was put out for him on our flat roof and he spent hours there, studying his Bible meditating, planning. It was there that he conceived the idea that the hill opposite the north wall was in reality Golgotha, the 'Place of the Skull'". She also says: 'He was not very tall, and had fair, curly hair, and I remember how blue his eyes were, and the blue double-breasted suit he wore. I did not know General Gordon was famous, only that he was my friend and I loved him.' At the Garden Tomb, we look across to the original Spafford Home on the city walls, sometimes sharing this story with our visitors. Even though Gordon was not the first to identify an alternative site for Golgotha from the Church of the Holy Sepulchre, he made a strong case for its significance.

I have also had the opportunity to work for short periods in Southern Sudan after the Interim Peace Agreement was signed in 2005, living alongside Christians there. Ironically, many refugees from South Sudan have sought sanctuary here in Israel as refugees from Egypt. Appreciating the sad condition of that land, its history and the many challenges faced by the newly created nation of South Sudan, perhaps the faith and heroism of General Charles Gordon can inspire a new generation there.

I have reproduced the words, abbreviations and expressions used by Gordon in his letters exactly as written.

Rosalind Meryon

The Garden Tomb, Jerusalem
April 2012

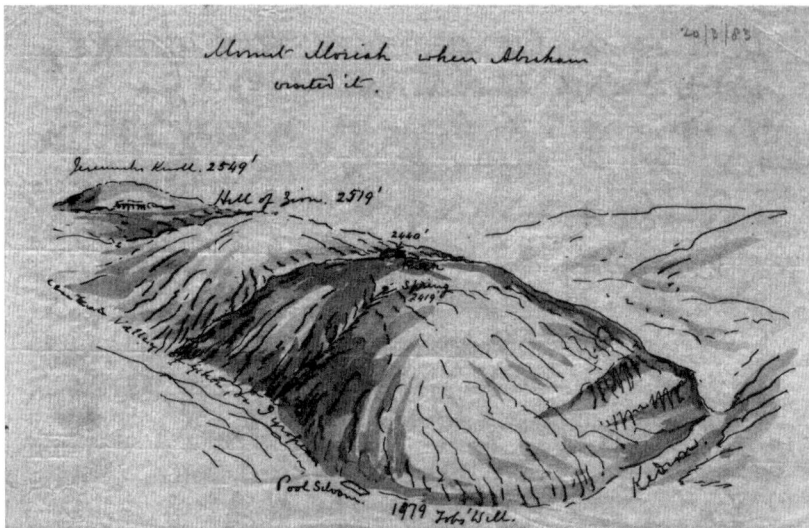

MOUNT MORIAH WHEN ABRAHAM FIRST VISITED IT

«*Rosalind Meryon provides readers with a fascinating compilation of letters written in 1883 by the famous soldier General Charles George Gordon. Gordon was not just a military man, but held deep religious convictions and had a passion for trying to understand the topographical layout of biblical Jerusalem. These letters are a marvellous insight into his world.*» **(Dr Shimon Gibson, University of the Holy Land, Jerusalem)**

Our thanks to those who have encouraged and advised in this project:

Rev. Victor Jack, Chairman of Trustees,The Garden Tomb Association,

Father Jean-Michel Tarragon, Archivist, Ecole Biblique, Jerusalem

Dr Shimon Gibson,The University of the Holy Land, Jerusalem

Mr Michael Critchley, Day Three Editions, Liskeard, Cornwall, UK

Ms Rebekah Kosinski, Graphic designer, Garden Tomb, Jerusalem

INDEX

Editor's Note	III
Introduction	VII
Biography of Gordon	1
Letters written November 1882	5
Letter to Gordon's sister 18/1/1883	6
Letter to Sir John Cowell 20/1/1883	9
Letter to Sir John Cowell 5/3/1883	10
Letter to Sir John Cowell 8/3/1883	18
Letter to Sir John Cowell 20/3/1883	30
Letter to Sir John Cowell 27/4/1883	31
Notes on Gibeon Illustrated	33
Letter to Sir John Cowell 7/5/1883	35
Letter to Sir John Cowell 25/5/1883	39
Plan of Latrun-Emmaus Baptistry	40
Notes to Accompany Letters without Dates	41
Site of Temple	45
More Notes on Golgotha	47
Zechariah on Outflow of Waters	50
Excerpt from Undated Letter	51
East Hill of Zion resembling Human Form	52
West Hills of Zion	57
Passages on Pools and Conduits	58
The Potters' Field	59
Plan of Solomon's Temple	60
Index	62
Appendix PEF article April 1885	66
Gordon's Diagrams & Photographs	

LETTERS FROM JERUSALEM 1883

Introduction

These are a collection of letters written by General Charles Gordon, an eminent British Army officer and archetypal Victorian hero, who visited Palestine in 1883. They were sent to a friend, Sir John Cowell, Comptroller of the Household of Queen Victoria. These letters, an account of a military engineer, tactician, Biblical scholar and devout Christian man make a unique chronicle of his observations and deductions linking the Scripture, the local topography, together with his own faith at a time when Jerusalem was undeveloped beyond what we know as the Old City. His lively mind and energy in despatching the volume of correspondence Gordon sent out from the country to his sister, brother and Sir John Cowell, amongst others is impressive. The letters are unedited, but annotated with some additional punctuation, to demonstrate the flow of ideas of this man and give us fresh understanding of events two to four thousand years earlier.

Today, Jerusalem is a busy and modern city, with two cultures and three religions determining its character. Millions of pilgrims visit the country of Israel, a nation only since 1948, to visit holy places and to see the sites from so many centuries of history and consider the tragic consequences of war and destruction. At the Garden Tomb, we average quarter of a million visitors each year who come to see the ancient tomb, which some archaeologists confirm is from the Second Temple period. This tomb could be the site of the Resurrection of the Lord Jesus Christ, with features that match the eye witness gospel accounts. The site is occasionally marked on maps: 'Gordon's Tomb' beside 'Gordon's Golgotha'. The land was finally purchased in 1894 with a money raised by an appeal in the London 'Times' after it came up for sale in 1892. The adjacent escarpment, on the same geological fold as Mount Moriah, or the Temple Mount, with the clear image of a huge human skull in the rock face, convinced General Gordon along with others that this was the actual site of the Crucifixion.

Golgotha - "The Place of the Skull", had been a Jewish place of stoning in pre-Roman times and the gospel of John tells us that: "At the place where Jesus was crucified, there was a garden, and in the garden was a new tomb cut out of solid rock in which no-one had ever been laid." (John 19: 41 NIV)) This tomb belonged to a member of the Jewish ruling council, and a secret disciple of Jesus, Joseph of Arimathea. The public response for funds to purchase the Garden Tomb was a form of memorial to the man whose tragic death in Khartoum came just one year after his sojourn in Jerusalem. The Garden is maintained by a British charitable trust, The Garden Tomb Association which bought these letters at auction in 1947 from the family of Sir John Cowell. Together with the diagrams and photographs sent by General Gordon, we believe that these should be made available for all to see and may help some to gain insights, not only into the character of this extraordinary man, but also to their own faith and understanding of the events that "changed the world" one spring weeked in the first century AD.

General Charles George Gordon 1833 – 1885

Charles George Gordon was born on January 28th, 1833 into a military family at Woolwich, where his father, General H.W Gordon, Royal Artillery, was inspector of the carriage department. Fourth child of a lively and large family, the young Charles became commissioned into the Royal Engineers in June 1852, and in 1854, as a second lieutenant, was posted to Pembroke Dock, where his faith became reality under the influence of a "very religious captain of the 11th". Gordon was sent to Balaklava in the Crimea and arrived there in January 1855, where he distinguished himself in the siege of Sevastopol as an exceptionally enterprising, intelligent and courageous young officer.

'Chinese' Gordon

After returning to England, he was promoted to Captain in April 1859 and volunteered for service in China. He was present at the occupation of Peking and the destruction of the Summer Palace there. He contracted smallpox in 1862 and wrote then: "I am glad to say that this disease has brought me back to the Saviour." In April 1863, British troops, commanded by General Charles Staveley were sent to protect the European settlement in Shanghai from the T'ai P'ing rebels, who had overrun the rich central provinces, captured Nanking and threatened European trading at Shanghai. Citizens there had commissioned an American adventurer, F.T. Ward, to raise an army composed of peasants and the "riff-raff" to defend the city headed by European adventures and optimistically called "The Ever-Victorious Army". Ward was killed soon afterwards and another American was appointed and soon dismissed when Gordon, an acting Major, was appointed to command this 'irregular' army. In the next 18 months, he proved himself to be unusually gifted in heading such a motley group and turned them into a disciplined and effective fighting force. Time and time again they crushed superior numbers of opponents by Gordon's use of cunning and initiative and twice quelled mutinous action, by his will-power and personality. His bravery when found at the site of greatest danger, armed only with a light cane, became known to the superstitious soldiers as "Gordon's wand of victory". Gordon refused the many rewards offered to him by the Emperor, and since he had spent his pay on comforts for his troops, "left China as poor as I entered it."

Gravesend Gordon

He returned home in January 1865 to more tributes and fame, he refused invitations from political ministers and generals showered on him and he even destroyed the diaries of his Chinese exploits to avoid legends being made about him, but would from then on be referred to as "Chinese Gordon". He was promoted to Lt. Colonel, made a Companion of the Bath, a decoration for distinguished civil servants and in September 1865 was appointed as the Commander of the Royal Engineers at Gravesend. There, he spent much of his time and money on looking after the street urchins whom he fed, clothed and taught with the assistance of his housekeeper and friends, placing them in employment, many in the merchant ships that sailed up and down the nearby River Thames. These 'boys' became his family and he would keep in touch with most of them for the rest of his life. In a desire to reach other disadvantaged folk with the simple, yet profound, message of the gospel for the poor he printed and distributed Christian tracts, even distributing them out of railway trains to workers. He studied the Bible closely each day, yet never became part of a denomination or sect and was regarded with suspicion by the more affluent members of Victorian society.

Governor Gordon of Equatoria

In September 1872, Gordon was appointed by Gladstone's Liberal government to a commission held on the Danube. After a chance meeting in Constantinople (present day Istanbul) with the Prime Minister of Egypt, Gordon was offered the post of Governor of Equatoria, insisting that his salary should be reduced from that of his predecessor, Sir Samuel Baker, from £20,000 to £2000. This province extended from the Egyptian Sudan, (now Northern Sudan) down the Nile to the still uncharted south, where there was no existing form of central government. The Khedive of Egypt profited from the flourishing slave trade in the area. This time was one of intense strain and hard work for the new Governor, but his endurance and speed on camelback became legendary in the two and a half years of service there. He succeeded in establishing a line of 'stations' to the frontier with Uganda and in denting the slave trading business, much to the chagrin of the local tribal dealers and the Egyptian governor of Sudan. Most of his staff succumbed to fatal illness or became incapacitated by disease whilst Gordon remained healthy and vigorous. Gordon returned to England on Christmas Eve in 1876, but after much hesitation agreed to resume service with the Khedive only if he were appointed as Governor General of the Sudan with the Equatorial Province. "I go up alone, with an infinite Almighty God to direct and guide me," he wrote home. In May 1876, he was installed in Khartoum and carried out sweeping administrative reforms in a few days, then left for Darfur with 300 men to tackle a rebel army of 3,000 men, riding into the camp alone except for a small escort and an interpreter; this so impressed the warriors that half of them left to join Gordon's force and the rest retreated. He pursued the slave traders of Darfur again in 1879 and with the help of the Italian aide, Romolo Gessi, finally crushed the revolt. Due to the burdens of office, loneliness, the ongoing struggle with stamping out slave trading, malaria, exhaustion from frustration with the Egyptian Government, Gordon resigned from office and sailed for England in January 1880.

Gordon in China, South Africa and Palestine

In May 1880, Gordon accepted the post of Private Secretary to the Viceroy designate of India, the Marquess of Ripon, but then resigned soon after reaching India. Two days later, he accepted an invitation from Sir Robert Hart, Inspector General of Customs in Peking to return to China. There, he, with his unique style of working with rebel groups, convinced his old friend Li Hung Chang not to oppose the government, and then dissuaded the Grand Council of China from embarking on war with Russia in bold and undiplomatic style. By December 1880, Gordon was back in England and during a visit to the Rector of Tywell, in Northamptonshire, experienced a spiritual regeneration. From this time participating in taking Holy Communion became very important in his life and seemed to calm his somewhat irascible and unpredictable nature. From April 1881 until April 1882, he was Commander of Royal Engineers in Mauritius, becoming intrigued by its possible location as the Garden of Eden. From there, Gordon travelled to the Cape Colony, South Africa, where he reorganised the colonial forces. He visited Basutoland (now Lesotho) where he saved the life of a colleague, and his own, by his "mesmeric influence, quite inexplicable in scientific terms". His memorandum on the Basuto people became the basis for the eventual reconstruction of the region as an imperial protectorate. In November 1882, on returning to England and refusing an invitation from King Leopold to assume command in the Belgium Congo, he departed for Palestine for a time of rest and study, where this correspondence begins. Following the last of these letters and notes, Gordon left Jerusalem for Jaffa on the coast in July, 1883, having established in his own mind the true Biblical sites. His prodigious correspondence continued, but not to Sir John Cowell that we have record of. In December, Gordon embarked for Europe.

A Glorious 'Martyrdom' and the final Mission to Sudan

In January, 1884, Gordon was in Brussels considering again King Leopold's invitation and resigning his military commission. Meanwhile, an obscure mystic had announced himself as the 'Mahdi', the Expected One, who would restore the faith of Islam by initiating a Holy War. A British expeditionary force, in support of the Egyptian Khedive's government was sent out but in November 1883, its leader, Colonel Hicks, and his entire army were surrounded and slaughtered by the Mahdi's dervishes. Gladstone's government in London, having determined to evacuate and abandon Sudan, were forced, largely by public opinion, to step in and invited Gordon to assist them. Unfortunately, their aims and objectives were far from clear, with confusion as to whether this was an advisory mission, or to re-establish government in Khartoum, or to evacuate the Sudan. Gordon reached Khartoum on February 18th, 1884 where with the approval of the Khedive and by recommendation of the British Consul General, Sir Evelyn Baring, he was re-commissioned as Governor General of Sudan. He succeeded in evacuating 2.000 women, children and the sick or wounded before the forces of the Mahdi closed in on the town. From this time, the procrastination of the British government to requests for reinforcements, and relief for the man whom they had despatched to achieve the impossible, made disaster inevitable. The siege started on March 13th, but not until August did pressure from the British public, and Queen Victoria herself, promote some action in relieving the siege of Khartoum. However, it was not until November that a relief force under Lord Wolseley set out from Egypt. The resistance of Khartoum, under attack and starvation until January 26th, is one of the formidable achievements of this unusual military commander whose skill, energy and unquenchable spirit, without staff or companions, inspired the local people and the few remaining Egyptian soldiers garrisoned there. The delay of the relief force encouraged the Mahdi's troops to make a final assault on a gap in the ramparts caused by the fall of the Nile. The garrison was butchered and Gordon met his assailants on the staircase of the Governor's Quarters wearing a white uniform, red tarboosh, left hand resting on his sheathed sword and made no effort to defend himself. A spear was flung at Gordon's chest; he fell forward on the stairs where others pressed to stain spears in this blood. His head was cut off and taken to the Mahdi. The relief force arrived two days too late.

The slight, wiry looking, brave, unorthodox Christian disciple, with the clear, blue eyes and with an apparent magical influence in his life soon became a legend both in the Sudan and in the land of his birth.

R.A.M. 2012

The Deputy Adj. General

Address 5 Rockstone Place, Southampton

15 11 82

Sir,

I have the honour to request that you will submit for formal consideration for HRH the Field Marshal Cmg[1] . In chief this, my application for leave to travel in Belgium the Ionian Isles, and Palestine.

I have the honour to be,

Sir,

Your most obedient Servant,

CE Gordon

Major General (from a letter given recently to the Garden Tomb)

Southampton 9. 11. 82

My dear Cowell,

Thank you for you kind letter.

I arrived yesterday, and am going to Palestine at end of month I hope, if they will not let me go then, I shall go to Corfu or thereabouts.

Old Smithy whom I saw as I left Cape Town quite remembered you. He was pleased you remembered him. I hope Mrs Cowell, Lady Cowell, your family and the Bradons are well. Mrs Bradon has been very kind to my sister, thank her for it.

Believe me,

Yours sincerely,

C G Gordon

---

[1] Prince George, Duke of Cambridge (George William Frederick Charles; 26 March 1819 – 17 March 1904) was a member of the British Royal Family, a male-line grandson of King George III. The Duke was an army officer and served as commander-in-chief of the British Army from 1856 to 1895. He became Duke of Cambridge in 1850.

FROM GENERAL GORDON'S LETTER TO HIS SISTER

18th January, 1883

I walked round the city, about two hours quiet walking, then went in and saw the so-called Pool of Bethesda[2] ; also the Wailing Place of the Jews[3]. A Mohammedan (?) gave me the Psalms in Hebrew and English, open at the sixty-ninth. I read it, and it seemed wonderful how the Jews, who were kissing the stones with the greatest emotion, could not see the parallel between our Lord and the Messiah. The Jews were His church, and they are now undergoing His crucifixion.

I feel convinced that the hill near the Damascus Gate is Golgotha. From it you can see the Temple, the Mount of Olives, and the bulk of Jerusalem; quite pools of blood are lying there. It is covered with tombs of Muslim; there are many rock-hewn caves; and gardens surrounding it. Now, the place of execution in our Lord's time must have been, and continued to be, an unclean place as long as the Jews held their state. The Muslim would consider such a place unclean, and it is evident the Crusaders never built on it; so, to me, this hill is left bare ever since it was first used as a place of execution, and it never can be used till the Muslim leave the country, as it has tombs on it. The little hill on the side would be just the place where the women would look on afar off, ready to run away by the road if molested. It is very nice to see it plain and simple, instead of having a church built on it.

I am going to see a house three miles from Jerusalem; for there are none to let on the Mount of Olives ... I have found a house at Ein Kerem. It is surrounded by barren, rocky hills, and will be solitary enough.

It is quite unnecessary to come to Palestine; just read the Scriptures in their simple words, for no-one could describe it better. Put yourselves in the actors' skin, and you will feel as Peter and the others did, and know their motives.

General Sir J. Cowell KCS   Hotel Jaffa Gate,

---

[2] Probably the Birket Israin
[3] The Western Wall

Jerusalem, 20.1. 83

Windsor Castle.

My dear Cowell,

When I arrived here, I asked about the Urtas[4] property, from a Mr Wiseman Ch. M. S,[5] who knows the Marshalams[6] , he had never heard of your property but said the M. Family (father of your man and others of the same family) were living at Urtas in their own house and also, that as far as he knew, the old house of M. who was killed, was in ruins and the land in hands of Turks. I consequently did not go there, but have got a house at Ain Karim, St John's[7] 3 miles W of Jerusalem for 6 months. I spoke to N J Moore H M C[8] here about the land, and told him what I had heard, also of the Turkish law that of property is not cared for, for 10 years it lapses to the Turkish Crown. He says he has a hazy idea that he has seen some paper about your purchase of land and that the Turkish govt. could not take it unless they had primarily referred to him. I told him, I would tell you, and that you would write to him about it. I also when I get settled, will go and see about it and let you know. From what I have seen of the Dwellers Jerusalem, I would not trust them very much, and perhaps the Marshalam family have absorbed your property, leaving the ruins of house. I have been over the best part of Jerusalem. It is very interesting, but I think anyone can now realize the sacred history as well in England as here, the reproach is the same if we want to follow Him, we must suffer that reproach. He was called <u>mad, impious, unsettling men's minds, misleading the people, the friend of publicans & sinners,</u> always with them, <u>breaking of their idea of ceremonial law,</u> unclean, possessed by <u>an unclean devil, wine bibber, glutton,</u> working miracles, by Satan's agency, it is a very hard thing, but, to the degree we have this reproach, so as we approach Him, and His likeness.

You have the ordnance map of Jerusalem[9], look at the shape of the contour 2459[10] Jeremiah's grotto near Damascus Gate. It is in the shape of Skull, near it are gardens, & caves it is close to many roads, and close to it are the shambles of Jerusalem. 200 yds from it to the W. is a heap of ashes, calcified bone

---

[4] Artas. 4 kilometres .SW of Bethlehem
[5] CMS, The Church Missionary Society
[6] Probably the Meshullam family who farmed near Artas
[7] Ein Kerem today, birthplace of John the Baptist, by tradition
[8] Noel Temple Moore, British Consul
[9] Charles Wilson, conducted an Ordnance Survey of Jerusalem mapping in 1864
[10] See Map 17

and bits of charcoal, this heap has been opened lately and large cisterns are found under it. **Numbers XIX** speaks of the Water of separation, Red Heifer ashes and the contour is 2538. To me this Jeremiah's grotto Hill is the site of the crucifixion. Others have also said so. The outstretched arms embrace Mount Olives & all Jerusalem. *"All day long I have stretched out my arms to a disobedient and gain saying people."* He was crucified at the time of the morning sacrifice, 9 am and died at the time of the evening sacrifice, 3 pm, 6 hours, (6 days work). I hour rest on Cross whilst Joseph went to get leave from Pilate to take the body.

The knob of land, to the East of the skull shaped contour which is numbered 2529 near tomb is just where the women would look from far off, so as to be ready to run with the passers- by in the road if they were molested. The south from Pilate's Praetorium seems to this place near, and it would seem much more appropriate site than that of the Holy Sepulchre Church. I reason also, that the Golgotha of time of our Lord was unclean to Jews of that time, and would not be built upon, that it remained so with the Muslims except for tomb and so the place left intact to this time. The pools of blood at the slaughter house on the side of the hill also would be preventative of any buildings being ever erected there. However, you may know more about it, than I do. If you look at map and find Kobebeh[11], alias Emmaus, you will see that the road to it leads from Damascus Gate and no roads lead to it from the Jaffa Gate which is the gate nearest to Holy Sepulchre Church. One can imagine how Peter and Cleopas hung about the place of crucifixion and Joseph's Cave near Jeremiah's Grotto all the day of resurrection, and then went off towards Emmaus at dusk, fearing to go to Bethany.

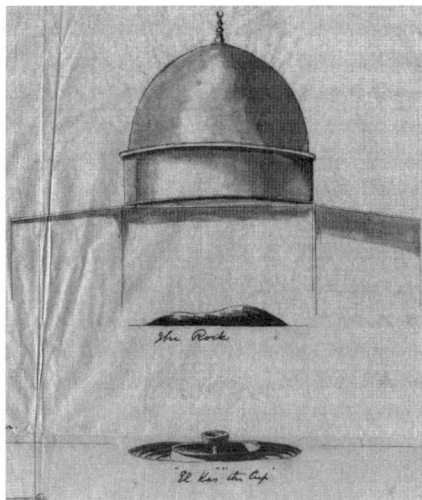

Goodbye. I hope Lady Cowell, your children and you are well. I will write again soon. Excuse this scrawl.

Believe me yours sincerely,

C G Gordon.

DOME OF THE ROCK

---

[11] Al-Qubeiba, 11 kilometres NW of Jerusalem, a possible site of 'Emmaus'.

Jerusalem,

20.1. 83

My dear Cowell,

I send you some sketches of Temple and Golgotha. Willie Anderson will send you the notes which accompany them. I hope you & Lady Cowell are well. This is a splendidly interesting land. I have a home 3 miles from Jerusalem. There will be a great row if Jeremiah's grotto is found to be the true Golgotha for the Holy Catholic Church will say their clergy have disowned them. However they will never be able to spoil the hill over the Jeremiah grotto. For it is a Turkish Cemetery.

SKETCH OF HILL OVER JEREMIAH'S GROTTO LOOKING SOUTH CONTOUR OF WHICH RESEMBLES SKULL

Yours sincerely,

C G Gordon

My dear Cowell,

Thanks for your kind letter, which encourages me to inflict another on you.

Either the Caliph who erected Mosque Omar, or 'The Dome of the Rock', and made the Fountain 'El Kas' , knew through some Jew of the dimensions of the Temple and size of the Brazen Altar, or he hit off the size very closely.

Take the Mosque Dome of the Rock, and the Sanctuary

The outer court Temple was 100 cubits, the width of the Mosque is ditto, height of the Porch 60 cubits, height of Mosque 61 or 97 ft. You know the old form of apse.

The Protestant church apse pushed it up against the wall.

The original apses were dome covered and the Caliph made a full Dome (query may it not have been the plan of the Constantine church, but I do not think it). I will not press the heights, for it is not certain that the Porch was 60c only it is said to be likely to have been double the height of the Holy Place, which is supposed to be 30 cubits. I will only stand out for the Place. As for the Temple Altar, it was 10c., that of the Tabernacle 3c., the size of the Temple was 20 x 20 by 10 high, that of the Tabernacle altar was 5 x 5 x 3 high, why was not height of Temple Altar 4 x 3 = 12c. I think the missing two c. were made up by the Ark itself, I send you the sketch made accurately from big plan & you will see yourself.

The Rabbis declared the rock was the nucleus when the world was as it were, spread out, that on it Adam was made of that flesh coloured earth, and that from thence, he was put into Eden *"and in it"* (the Garden)*"He placed the man."* The Brazen Sea is 10 cubits in diameter & it is said to be placed *"on the right side of House eastwards over against the South."* **1 Kings VII 38**[12] on right side of house over against the South. **2 Chronicles III. 10,** it is to contain 2000 Baths. Whether the Fountain does contain that quantity, I do not[13] for I have not its exact dimensions, & there is a doubt about the Bath. El Kas means the chalice or bowl and it is the term used by Arabs for our sacramental chalice.

I next call your attention to the washing place being opposite to the "cup".

Now it is certain that the Brazen Sea or Laver was first utensil used in 'Jewish church', that it is the Font of our Christian church, we have the Table of the Lord which was and is the Altar at which we offer ourselves willing sacrifices to God. The Holy of Holies and Holy Place have risen, for Christ is the Holy of Holies in where we meet God and through the torn flesh, we offer our prayers. It is remarkable how in our churches, the contents of the Ark of the Covenant are placed over the Table of the Lord by the 10 Commandments ostentatiously placed and that we can look in them without fear. In fact, it is quite in accordance with Scripture that the Sanctuary should be no longer on earth & that only the Altar and Laver should be here. It is odd that the Rock & Fountain above should be, as I think, in the Temple area. Take the old Temple as our Modern Church.

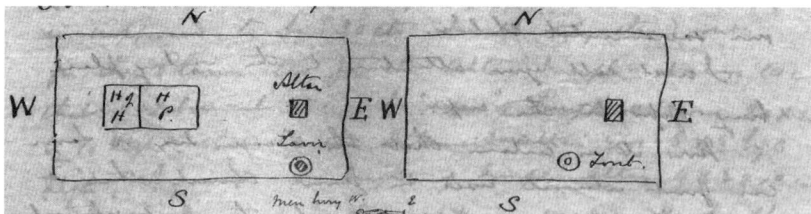

Since the giving of the Holy Ghost, it would seem that our bodies are the Sanctuaries and in our Church occupy the site of the Sanctuary of Israel. However, it may be certainly of the Jewish Ritual we have two utensils, viz. the Table of the Lord same name as Malachi calls the Altar (Malachi 1:7), for Baptism, or Laver, and it is remarkable that the Jews wail towards the true Font or site of Brazen Sea.

---

[12] I Kings 7: 39
[13] Possibly omitted 'know'

11

Another odd thing is that the El Kas is about 200 cubits from the centre of the Rock. I have not gone into details, as to thickness of walls, & now I have put the Porch on Temple. You will see the site of the Sanctuary is not close over the steps. The N. part is covered by the little house, there keeper of the Dome of the Rock sleeps. Wilson, however, thinks with Fergusson[14] that the site is in the SW angle, but how does he get over the unsightly rock which unless it was kept for the Altar can surely be supposed to be left. I call your attention the 'Cisterns of the Sea'[15] close to the 'Cup' or 'El Kas'. Why are they called cisterns of the Sea?

As for the Grotto, Jeremiah's,[16] the ash heap that has been opened, nothing more has been done as yet. The little church[17] whose base they have opened out is mainly square, & has a Greek inscription, therefore, it cannot be the Church put up by Crusaders, whom they found they had not funds to rebuild the large church of Empress Theodosia[18]. The history as far as I know is this. Empress Theodosia erected in the 4th Century, a church to St Stephen outside the Damascus Gate. It was destroyed by Chrosous[19] in 606 or thereabouts. The Crusaders in 1100 AD found the site and not having money to rebuild it, made a small one alongside.

On approach of Saracens, then the Crusaders dismantled it, as it could aid the enemy[20], this is state of affairs, when the ash heap is opened outside the Damascus Gate and a small church A. nearly square with Greek inscriptions is found, and two huge pillars and a portion of a large church B. near to it[21].

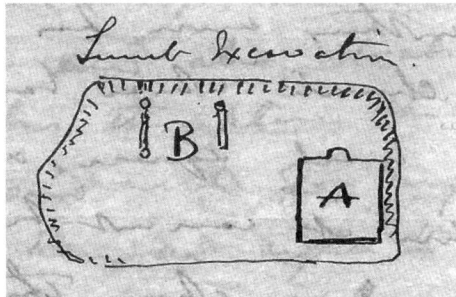

---

[14] Charles Wilson and James Fergusson
[15] The Great Sea – large cistern Bahr-el-Kebir on the North side of the El Aqsa mosque
[16] South of the Grotto and close to the City wall, a conduit was measured by Conrad Schick and plan published of it.
[17] Now the property of the Ecole Biblique
[18] This was the Empress Eudocia, not Theodosia
[19] Chrosoes II Persian invasion of Palestine c 614 when many Byzantine Holy Places were destroyed
[20] Church restored by Crusaders in 1099 was destroyed by them in 1187 to deprive Saladin's army of a strong point in the city.
[21] Now part of Ecole Biblique and Church of St Stephen/St Etienne, dedicated in 1900

Arculf[22] says in 680 AD, he saw the church over Sepulchre, the Church Virgin, the Church Golgotha on Knoll and Basilica over place where crosses was found, he says that these were erections of Constantine and places them thus, see next page, and he says the Church over Sepulchre had these walls.

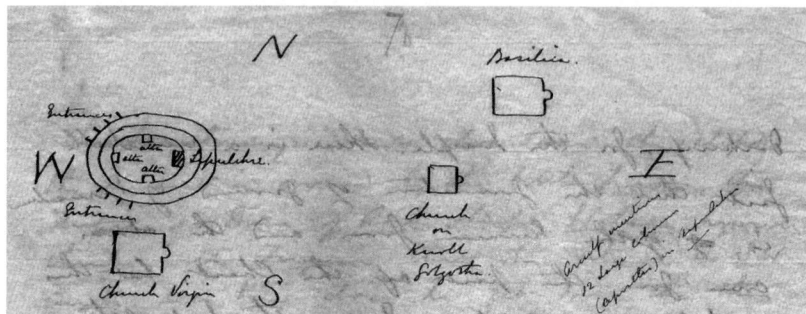

Church on Knoll Golgotha

Arculf mentions 12 large columns (apostles) in sepulchre

Query: is the disinterred Church the church of Virgin? It cannot be the Church of Crusaders, for it has a Greek inscription which the French Consul has sent to Paris, where it may be deciphered[23], I would like to copy it, but they are jealous about it and it is covered with mud. I wrote to Baron De Avril[24] to try and get him to get the 7000 £ necessary to buy the land up to the Slaughter house, but I can see that the French Consul, an old friend of mine, is under Priestly rule and would not like to find the Sepulchre here. Russian Consul General tells me that in the picture of crucifixion, by French Painter Jerome, he writes under it, 'Damascus Gate'.

The Victims were found & slain on N. of the Altar.

Near Jeremiah's Grotto are the huge Quarries where the Temple stone were shaped out in darkness for the Temple[25]. There is a remarkable fact that the formation of ground of Jerusalem is of the human form, and the stones came from the part of the Chest, but this is between ourselves. To use the fact of the Shew Bread Table being on N., the victims of which He was the true one, being led & slain on N. goes a great way.

---

[22] A German Bishop, who toured the Middle East in late 7th Century and an observer of the rise of Islam.

[23] Not clear text

[24] Text unclear

[25] Solomon's Quarries, so called , now known as the Cave of Zedekiah

I see scarcely anyone, from week to week. I go up to a hill near here, nearly as high as Neby Samwil[26], ancient Mispah[27] and from where I can see the sea and Jaffa and also, Moabite sites & Jerusalem & Bethlehem and also the place where the Ark was neglected for so long, and wish for my exodus. For somehow I feel have no right to be selfishly idle. Ebenezer must have been here about 2 miles from the place which is Bethcar[28]. A huge wady runs down here to the sea, though which Philistines used to come & did come when Samuel took that suckling lamb. I am sure the hailstones here are enough to drive back any army. I get inbred with Scripture history, never think of anything else and same post as brought your letter, brought one from Seychelles, asking me to do something for the poor Sultan of Perak[29] in whom I was interested and about whom I shall write to Lysple......[30] Stanley, so will not trouble you, I suppose you know he is there for Bink's Murder, he was never tried & it is a question, for it was now owing to Bink's indiscretion in a private way, that he was killed. The case reminded me of the Amalekite slave left behind at Ziglag marauding party who gave information to David, & led to their destruction; mindlessness in little matters bring heavy retribution on men and nations.

The Jews of present day say that Jeremiah's grotto is the Beth ha Sakhilah, or "Place/House of Stoning" of old time and that by Talmud, it must have been a precipice. If you look at the Bible Dict[31] Truth you will see original of the Plan, Jerusalem XII century, under head "Jerusalem" showing Stephen's gate, the Damascus Gate, and Stephen's church outside. Odd that they marked Golgotha where they have, but we must consider their church ideas. I wish a good Painter would paint the scene there. The High Priest mocking said amongst themselves with the Scribes, *"He saved others etc."* **Mark XV. 31** does not imply that they must needs have been on the wall. They could have seen the hill from the same high place near the Temple. I believe most people now say the present wall at Damascus Gate is the second Wall. The third wall was built by Agrippa[32] after Crucifixion, I think City of David was N. of Temple & that Tyropoean[33] Valley is the "Gihon"[34], but I will not say why at present, for I get credit for fancies.

---

[26] The Arab name for the traditional tomb of Samuel north west of Jerusalem
[27] Or Mizpah
[28] Location unknown
[29] Possibly Perak in Malaysia
[30] Name illegible
[31] Probably Dictionary
[32] Herod Agrippa I 39 – 44 AD
[33] Cheesemakers' Valley in Greek, separated the Temple Mount from the Upper City
[34] Hebrew "bursting forth" Gihon is a spring which supplied water to the Temple area from underground

The formation of the ground on which Jerusalem is, when the debris is taken off, is wonderful, when taken into connection with the skull formation. If Adam was shaped like potters' clay in that Rock, then you & me were on it at the same time for we were in his loins. Did you ever notice **Micah VI. 5,6,7** from Balak's supplication **& 8,** Balaam's answer, it was very evil. Jerome[35] is the only Father who mentioned it in old times. I will go to Urtas next week & see myself & write you the state of affairs about land. Kindest regards to Lady Cowell & yourself. I like writing and making these sketches, only check me if I bore you.

Believe me,

Yours sincerely,

C G Gordon

PS I send you photograph of Jeremiah's Grotto, taken from the South.

If you want any more photos. Tell me, they are only a franc each so that is not much. You can see the Numbers on those I send you.

From the vicinity of Jeremiah's grotto is a conduit 3 feet wide, and sometimes 8 ft. high leading down to the Temple area near Tower Antonia[36]. You know the tradition that a subterranean river runs under Jerusalem & prophecy in Zechariah XIV about the water which will flow to the Mediterranean and the Dead Sea.

They are going to photo the Rock, I believe this year. I hope so.

Jesus wail before the Cup, my Brazen Sea, it is veiled to those, they who do not see it, they seek Baptism. They could not wait to enter the Holy of H. for without the Laver and Altar entry to H of H in death.

---

[35] St Jerome (c.347 – 420) or Hieronymus and translated the Hebrew text of the Old Testament into Latin.

[36] The fortress built by Herod the Great situated on the North West mount of the Temple area.

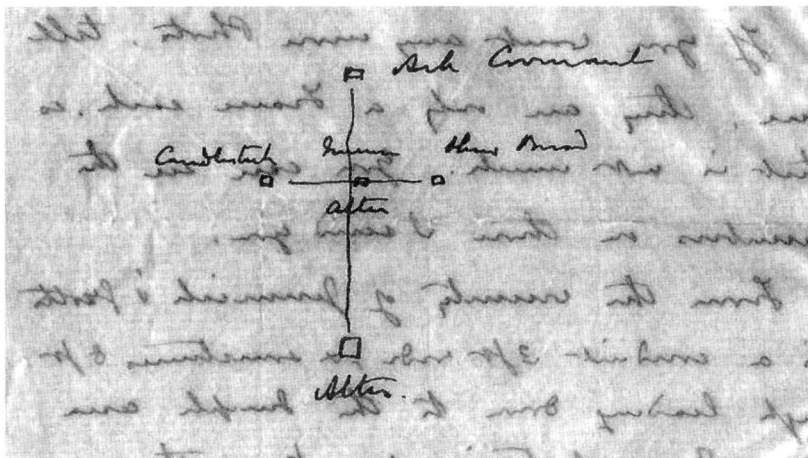

PS. It is very odd the Porch of the Sanctuary becoming steeper & going to W. of Holy of Holies in our church & the H. of H going over Altar.

Altar and Table of our Lord are synonymous terms and used by Jew, vide **Malachi**[37] , the place where God met man, they are not antithetical terms

---

[37] Malachi:1 10 - 12

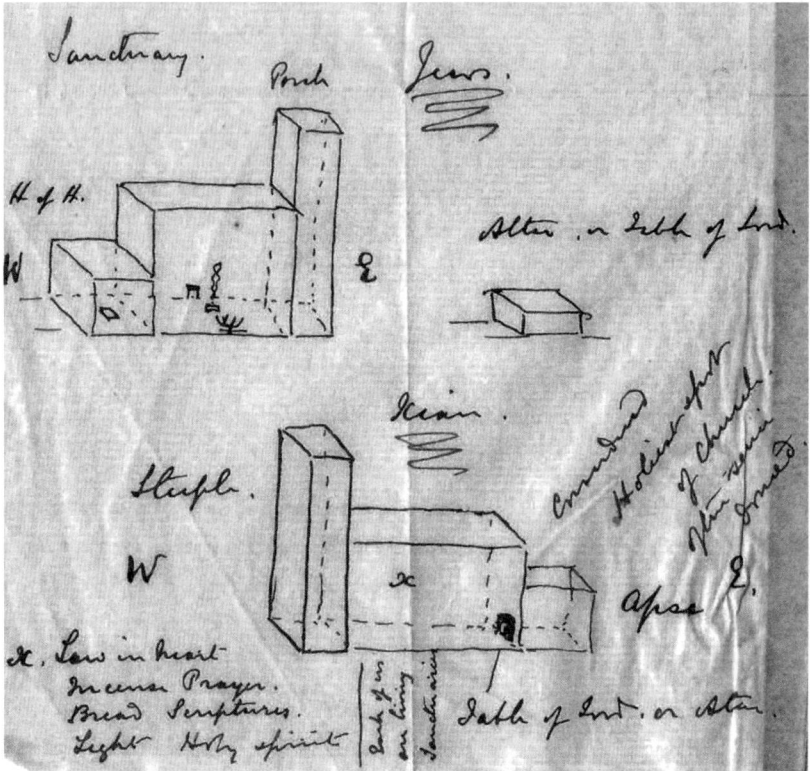

Law in Heart

Incense Prayer   **Each of us living sanctuaries**   **Table of Lord or Altar**

Bread Scriptures

Light Holy Spirit

Jerusalem,

8.3. 83

My dear Cowell,

I send you a big Golgotha, and also the Quarries where the stones of Temple were taken[38]. Christ is all in all. He is the key to the Scriptures. The victims were slain at north of Altar, therefore He was slain N of Jerusalem and Scripture goes out of its way, to tell us the hill was shaped like a skull. His church came from His side, His heart therefore, as the Temple, was a type of Him, the stones should be taken from a place corresponding to His heart. The streams of life giving water came from Him on the cross, so it is right we should find a corresponding conduit leading from the Cross.

Solomon's Temple was the outcome of man, it was Man's culminating fruit of Excellency and failed signally to keep man right, for Solomon's worship of other gods began in 20[39] year of reign, viz. 9 years after the Temple was completed, and 25 years after that, Shishak[40] pillaged it. Stephen says: "*Solomon built Him a House, howbeit the most High[41] not live in houses or temples made with hands. Heaven is my throne, earth my footstool, where is the place of my rest. My hands made all things.*"[42] "*He dwells with him that is of contrite and humble spirit, (thus saith the Most High, and lofty one that inhabiteth eternity whose name is Holy. I dwell in the High or Holy Place)*" **Isaiah LVII.14.**[43] Solomon's request was for wisdom to govern the people well, it was a worldly request, he was hard on the people, as Rehoboam found out, on his death, & when they rebelled. The quarries show that he was hard, for I doubt if these men were paid who worked there, many a sigh have these caverns heard. I therefore go back to say that I think the Temple of Solomon was typical of a self-righteous (good so far) man, not one stone is to be allowed to stay, Christ was and is the true Temple, but the Solomon's Temple is His type, and therefore must be like Him, its stones must be hewn out in tears and sorrow underground, as His living stones are.

I will just note down the line of thought I have in these matters, in order that you may understand me, and if you do not like the same then tell me and I will not bore you.

---

[38] Photos and diagrams, reproduced in this book
[39] Twentieth
[40] "In the fifth year of King Rehoboam, Shishak king of Egypt came up against Jerusalem" (1 Kings 14:25), now identified with Pharaoh Sheshonk
[41] Possibly missing word 'does'
[42] Acts 8:49
[43] Isaiah 57:15

I like the eating of the true knowledge of good and evil to be the root of our moral illness, and I think it is literally so, i.e. that by so eating Adam & all of us in him, became poisoned. Adam ate out of communion with God & consequently in union with Satan as communion means mutual understanding, so I believe Satan gave us his attitudes. I think that the prohibition was to the Body, for the soul could either eat, or not eat, that the sentence: *"Dust thou art, to dust will they return, for out the ground, was thou taken[44]"*. I think the soul is imputatively guilty by its oneness with the body of which it is the head. It is parallel to Christ, the Head of the Body the Church, imputatively made a curse for the sin of the Body His Church, imputatively considered guilty, using the Psalms as man does, I believe He initially felt as if He had committed those sins. What we lost by the Fall, Christ restored to us, where He had suffered for the broken Law, viz. the Holy Spirit to dwell in us. Wait, and He, for the Promise of My Father, of which ye have heard the Holy Ghost, was not yet given, as He was not yet glorified. We accept then that Christ bore the sin of His Body, the Church, and that He dowsed us with the indwelling of the Holy Spirit, and also before He ascended, gave us the antidote to the poison of the first communion with Satan, viz. His Body His Blood. *"Thou shalt not eat, the day thou doest, thou shalt surely die[45]"*. I also eat *"this is my body, my blood, whoso eateth my flesh and drinketh my blood hath eternal life[46]"*.

It is quite impossible not to see the analogy of these two eatings.

The two communions. 1. With Satan. 2. With God in Christ, the one in distrust of God, and trust in self: the other in distrust of self and trust of God. Neither do I believe that either is the first eating, we now (but in a slight degree) do we realize the sequences. I believe the Communion is great and grand remedy against our worldly failings, not immediate, but gradually, even as the effect of previous and remedies are gradual. In fact, I think the entry of Christ must need cause turmoil to the satanic family in us. I am not digressing as you will see. I recall the fact that I think the Body is the actual offender, the soul the imputatively guilty as being one with body, but no gifts could come to soul tell the majesty of the Law was indicated, therefore Christ came, and offered His Body, which suffered fully and completely, and on His ascension, enabled the gift of the Holy Ghost to be given us first in our souls which, having for sin of body, already died (been separated from God) each rise,(the first resurrection), and secondly (as we die in our bodies anticipatively) to the

---

[44] Genesis 3: 19
[45] Genesis 2:17
[46] John 6:54

body. I think both soul & body were dead, on our Lord's ascension, He gave the Holy Ghost which knit our souls to Him our Head and that by these souls then quickened, the mortal bodies are quickened . Our Lord's death gave birth to the Church, His body. His ascension gave the Church His Body His quickening Spirit. Our Lord's death raised our souls. His ascension have them the quickening spirit, by which our bodies are quickened after death, either anticipatively or actual. Nicodemus ignored the fact that between two births there must be a death[47]. Our bodies must die anticipatively or actually ere they rise.

Why was Tabernacle made? *"Make me a Sanctuary so that I may dwell amongst Israel.[48]"* The Sanctuary was made veiled in darkness, never but once a year to be entered and then only with blood, morning and night blood, blood, nothing but blood, without blood, no redemption, the blood is the life of the flesh. A sanctuary shut up and continual blood shedding, typical of the true sacrifice for the sins of the world, the Veil is rent and the Sanctuary disappears with all its shadows. No, not all the Altar and Laver stay with us, the Table of the Lord & and the Fruit, now it is very remarkable that the Altar of offering was the only utensil which needed atonement for itself; also that the days of its atonement were 7 days same as for man, without going into the question beyond saying, that I think the Sanctuary was the Head of man and the Altar is the body of man. I think that in the Altar we have the type of the Body. All the other utensils needed atonement because of the uncleanness of Israel, among whom they were. I shall not go into more now, for I expect you will see what I allude to, with respect to the hills of Jerusalem, viz. Jeremiah's grotto (Golgotha) Zion, and Mt. Moriah[49], the Head, Heart and Body. I felt sure of this, ere I came here.

This is my blood, the life is in the blood, show it to me, yet it is in the blood, so with the Wine. It is wine, yet it is His Blood, and in it is His eternal life. Parable Lazarus.[50] *"If they have not Moses & the Prophets, neither will they be persuaded if one rose from the dead."* Mark Lazarus[51]. He did rise from dead & they wanted to kill him for it, remarkable, the two names Lazarus.

In first eating, we in Adam eat together, in the second eating we, in union, eat together, before us the 10 Commandments were not shut up but displayed,

---

[47] John 3
[48] Exodus 25:8
[49] According to 2 Chronicles 3:1, the site of the Temple first constructed by Solomon
[50] Lazarus – the poor man in Luke 16:20 - 25
[51] John 11

our Table. We keep them in Christ. Do you know I felt sure that there ought to be a conduit from N. before I knew of it? Solomon's Pools flow from south, the Cup is supplied, drunk from them, they do not know whence the conduit. In plan I send you comes from, it is supposed to run under Jeremiah's grotto, neither is it known whence it goes into the Temple area. Odd that it passes in near the Gate of the Inspector. They dug out nearly all the Hill of Zion. I have made it a fine red. I shall send you some flesh coloured earth from Haram enclosure. The Pools of Blood close to the Skull are horrible, regular shambles, the bullocks and sheep instead of being butchered at altar, are butchered now, where I humbly believe He was butchered. They cannot make out the Greek inscription of the discovered church near "Golgotha" Damascus Gate, Bab el Amud, Gate of the "Pillar". I enclose a sketch of the ground on which Jerusalem stands, you can check it out from ordnance survey. Our "Golgotha" one can see by the Contours on the rock which is exposed, was once separated from Mt. Zion and by the little valley, the conduit was led from Jeremiah's Grotto to the Temple (the oesophagus, I call it). Titus would have had to cross the Tyropoean Valley (my Gehenna) had he attacked from Jaffa Gate, besides Josephus says he went to Camp of Assyrians which was on North, not west. I will try and get a plan of Jeremiah's Cave.

The state of spiritual life in old times, and now is shown by the Altars served. At the Altar we devote ourselves to this god or that, and that is the meaning of those altars Israel was always putting up. The sacrifices denote the god served of the god in self, then things pleasing to self, the god served etc. etc. The Jews kept on offering and offering, and more thought of the Almighty and the Holy of Holies and His ten words there, when they lost the Ark of the Covenant (which tradition says, Jeremiah hid in his grotto,) they say that a "Stone of Drinking" replaced it. Tacitus[52] and Josephus[53] say nothing was found in the H of H[54]. Our self judgement: Candlestick and light by which we walk our Incense table is self- approbation, our Show bread table is our opinion of the world as our guide. In reality after the Captivity, though outwardly, the Altars were set up to heathen gods, yet the Jew religion was formalism, the husk, & no kernel, they worshipped self and that under the name of the Almighty. At the Altars we eat with the Divinity, or idol, we serve and thus Paul alludes to the impossibility of being partakers of the table of Christ & that of idols.[55] Men like a dead God, one who will not interfere, and

---

[52] Publius Cornelius Tacitus (56 – 117 AD) was a Senator and historian of the Roman Empire
[53] Titus Flavius Josephus, (37 – 100 AD) also called Yosef ben Mattathyahu, was a Roman-Jewish historian
[54] Holy of Holies
[55] 1 Corinthians 8

one sees it here where all riches are expended on the churches & in a world which, when He was here, He was grudged even the ointments for his burial. Read Jeremiah's **Lamentations 1** in Septuagint[56] begins: *"And it came to pass that after Israel was taken Captive"*, and Jeremiah sat weeping and lamented with the lamentation was over Jerusalem, and said: (this not in our version. It seems likely that he was sitting down where the wall was broken down by the Chaldeans, near his grotto. The Jews now read these Lamentations on the date of destruction by Titus[57] and ......[58].; one can imagine him sitting in the Knoll, *"How doth the city sit solitary. Is it nothing to you who pass by, behold and see, if there be any sorrow like unto my sorrow, with which the Lord hath afflicted us in the day of His fierce anger,[59]"* just the words which would be thought of, by our Lord. *"Jerusalem spreadeth out her hands. All day long have I stretched out my hands, to a rebellious people."* Have you Wordsworth Commentaries, they are very good? Titus the Roman Eagle flew at the throat of Jerusalem, when he attacked at the Tower Hippicus[60]. You might ask quietly if sides of North alluded to in the **Psalm XLVIII** is literally in Hebrew 'Rib', it is very curious, if it is as Wordsworth says.

Though not necessary to salvation, the riches of the Scripture by knowledge of Greek and Hebrew it, the chief Prince of Meshech and Tubal, now the word chief there is Rosh, a proper name, & one of the Scythian tribes with Meshech & Tubal, and could be Russians, as Wordsworth says it is the only modern nation mentioned in the Old Testament by name, and Russia may be said only to have existed since Peter the Great[61]. Og, Gog, Magog, Agag are all words of our root "Pride" and "worldly power". The same word 'Rosh' is used for the summit of the Mt of Olives. Where David sent back Ark when he fled from Absalom, also for several reasons, Wordsworth gives, it is supposed the Ascension took place from Mt. Olives where the districts of Bethphage & Bethany meet, which could be at the Russian establishments on Mt. Olives: this connected with the large numbers of Russian Pilgrims is remarkable.

The word "skull", with reference to the Lord's crucifixion is repeated in 3 gospels. Now repetition, on a matter apparently so trivial, must have a

---

[56] The Ancient Greek translation of Hebrew Scriptures by seventy scholars, sometimes referred to as LXX

[57] Titus (39 –81), was Roman Emperor from 79 to 81. A member of the Flavian dynasty, commanded the Roman legions in sacking Jerusalem in 70AD. Titus succeeded his father Vespasian upon his death

[58] unclear

[59] Lamentations 1

[60] Near the present day Jaffa Gate

[61] Tsar of Russia, 1672 - 1725

meaning and when repeated means much. The prohibition, Thou shalt not eat, was only once given, the Eucharist is spoken in the Gospels & one epistle directly & in the other gospel indirectly, **John VI.** Paul on Hagar & Sarah[62], in a few words, open volumes to us. The two covenants, the two worlds, seen & unseen, matter and spirit. There is a repetition in this.

Temple	Altar	Onto congregation
Jerusalem	Temple	Palestine
Palestine	Jerusalem	Other nations of Earth
Other nations of earth	Palestine	All the created Spheres
All created Spheres	Earth	

You may say what good are these speculations, and I will tell you my thoughts. We all hate the shaping process to make us living stones, we hate being chipped in the dark, and often it is our enemies, or people we do not like who chip us, and to enable me to bear this chipping. I wish to see the reason of it and thus get light on the subject of my trials (which however, are light enough) I come to the conclusion that it matters little in what position I am in, so that get rid of self and that comforts me in lowly places. I think that to be 'A' governing huge countries, or 'B' occupying the smallest place are the same in reality, for Christ rules events as much in respect to A's government as He does in B's little affairs. A & B as far as the actual government are as flies in a fly wheel, these motions of actions are the only things which are of real import. Now every bush which leads man to see unseen things in the things seen, and to see analogy between the two, strengthens ones faith, in the belief that nothing is trivial, but that all things are important. It annoys me, lines of action which I take up, fail. It is, however, very comforting to think that the annoyance of it is ruled for God's purpose & also the failure of my attempts in any particular way. Then how one sees behind the scenes of life, events in Egypt are working in a way that human wisdom would not like, but I see in it, I think, the supporters of Allah tend, so in Ireland, things seem crooked, yet I believe they will come straight. To investigate these deep things as the Gnostics[63] did, and endeavour to bind them to give leave for a carnal life

---

[62] Galatians 4:21 - 28

[63] A segment of the early Christian church, who believed that special knowledge (gnosis) was a way to salvation

is bad, but to seek them in the communion with our Lord is good. Remember also that even the most trivial things are very important, that there is more than the eye sees in them, and in all the events of life. To me, it comforts me, to think we were all on that Rock in Adam, I do not feel so vexed with A & B. I also think that we have Palestine in us. Golgotha as well as the whole world, you in me, me in you, your sorrow is mine and vice versa. Taking a lower view it is better to study these matters, to steep one's mind in them, than to be picking at A, B & C back biting evil speaking, taking up reproach and being so terribly treacherous.

In Photo: Wailing place, you will see some small shrub growing out of the wall, I think it is the hyssop, it is a broom like plant, & would do so well for sprinkling. I shall try & get better insights made of the shape of the Cup & of the Rock.

Matthew, Mark & John speak of Golgotha, and explain the meaning. Place like a skull, Luke in our version AV has 'Calvary', now Calvary is from the Vulgate, and the proper exposition is Kranium "Cranium" in Greek testament, in which language it was written "the place which is called a skull". An ancient prophecy, Paul quotes. **Ephesians 5 V.14** *"Awake Oh Adam that sleepest, and Christ will touch thee"* and tradition says Adam was buried here, and that the blood from Christ the Lord, penetrated to his skull which is the reason a skull is often placed under Cross. It was a well -known place, for Evangelists to say **the Golgotha.** You see I have no paper, & am obliged to use ......[64] to a large extent. I am particularly interested in Gihon for it is one of the Paradise Rivers, and I dare say you have heard a tradition that says: sound of subterranean River is heard under Jerusalem. I enquired about it from two people, one my servant, another, a Muktar Musselman[65], just to hear what they had heard. They said that sounds of a river are often heard, & that someday a river will flow down valley of Fire[66] to Dead Sea, the Muslim said, that the noise is heard near these quarries on Fridays at noon. Both Xian servant & Muslim said that the River was to flow from direction of Damascus Gate; Zechariah XIV has a prophecy that in the latter days, Mt Olives will split asunder, also that, from Jerusalem, waters shall flow to Dead Sea & Mediterranean & shall cure Dead Sea. Monk at ......[67]. Said the valley should flow blood, from the armies around Jerusalem.

---

[64] Text indecipherable
[65] Head Man or notable Muslim
[66] Possibly Valley of Hinnom
[67] Text indecipherable

Madagascar

1. Tigris Adakkel

2. Euphrates

3. Gihon 'to burst forth' Heb

4. Pison 'to overflow' Heb

5. Havilah son of Joktam, brother Ophir, Sheba

That Indian Ocean was not submerged. That waters were heaped in store house in form of ice. That the rivers flowed into from their Heads into the Great River, not out of it, for if you think no 4 rivers flow out of one. Also I was 3 years at sources of Euphrates & Tigris & mountains of 6000ft separate these sources. Also a flood does not change much the forms of mountains, also Valley Arabah, Gulf Akaba are generally thought to be the bed of river; also Nile went into Bitter Lakes.

The boundaries of Red Sea, Persian Gulf & Indian Ocean, show a deep gulley along dotted line, and a vast basin 2600 feet deep at N of Madagascar.

Also **2 Peter III 5, 6, 7** says clearly:

World which then was, being overflowed with water finished.

World which now is, are kept in store, reserved for fire.

So that the old world, ante-diluvial, has finished being overflown with water.

Psalm XXXIII 7 *"He gathereth the waters of the sea in heaps and bringeth us depths in the storehouses."* When you have the catch word 'storehouses' and water can only be kept in heaps in form of ice, my belief the change of axis of earth caused flood, originally elispsis[68] & equator were in same place. Milton says; He bid His angels askance turn the axis of globe eccentric, so now you see why I am interested in Gihon and never will agree that Hinnom or Gihon were the same, it is odd Gihon means" bursting forth".

On Euphrates Babylon   all connected with the History of Israel

" Tigris   Nineveh

" Gihon   Jerusalem

"Pison   Egypt

Nilah in Sanskrit means Dark Blue, the Blue Nile from Lake Isana, Abbysinia. Godjam in the Province of Abbysinia, which is Havilah, in it is a great deal of gold. Gihon is said in our Version, "whole land Ethiopia", in the margin Cush. Cush was father to Nimrod who built Babylon, so the direction is good, but it is a petty ravine & and has no length. This is section of the Arabah and Akabah Valley and Gulf.

---

[68] Text unclear

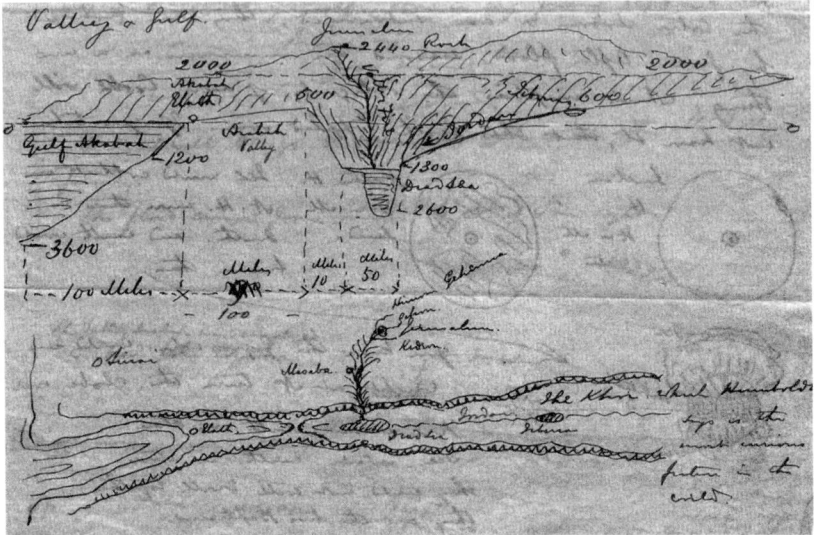

The Khive, which Humboldt says in the most curious feature in the world

I want to go down the Arabah Valley so as to fix the Watershed between the Dead Sea and the Gulf Akabah, some say it is a wall of chalk or marl, but they differ about height, some say it is 200ft almost perpendicular to North. If you know Canon Tristram[69], you might ask him, for I think he went there. As for the depression, Dead Sea, what do you say to a bed of Rock salt which got washed out at the time of Flood, remains of which are Gebel Uzdom, south end? Scripture does not say the Cities of Sodom are submerged, they were destroyed by fire. After flood, seasons are announced as a new thing, which implies the obliquity of axis. Cook will not have it that the earth tipped over. If you take S. Hemisphere it is all water. N. Hemisphere it is all land.

---

[69] Henry Baker Tristram

Ice would collect in the N. Hemisphere more than in South, and earth would become thus:

Southern H. It is all water   **Northern H. It is all land**

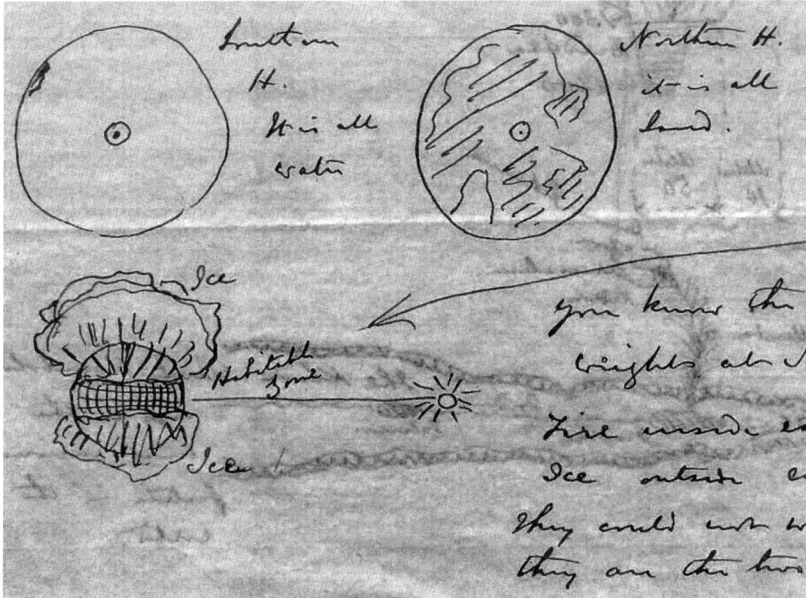

You know the gyroscope, would any weights at N turn the globe over. Fire inside the earth in store. Ice outside earth in store. They could not dwell well together, they are the two Baptisms.

There are many theories that Indian Ocean is submerged continent (Liguria), the way the Palms are distributed is remarkable. The mass of rivers flow N to S, the section of the globe is thus, the Ridge of high lands are to South, under tablelands of Russia and China.

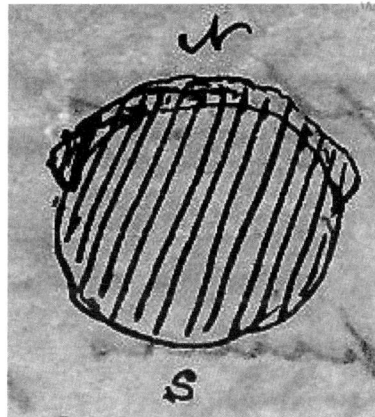

The Arabs consider Aden and neighbourhood, the cradle of race. I expect Aden is Eden, a District, the garden was a place selected in it. Seychelles is near the deep pond. Praslin is site of Garden. Mrs Bradon has seen a model of the Fruit. The other was Bread Fruit, only on one isle, 5 miles x 2 miles, does it grow. I will now conclude this terribly long letter with kindest regards to Lady Cowell and yourself. How is my good friend Elphin[70]?

Believe me
Yours sincerely,

C G Gordon.

PS I will try going to Urtas this week & see the Marshalam Family.

The flood came from direction of the N if I am right.

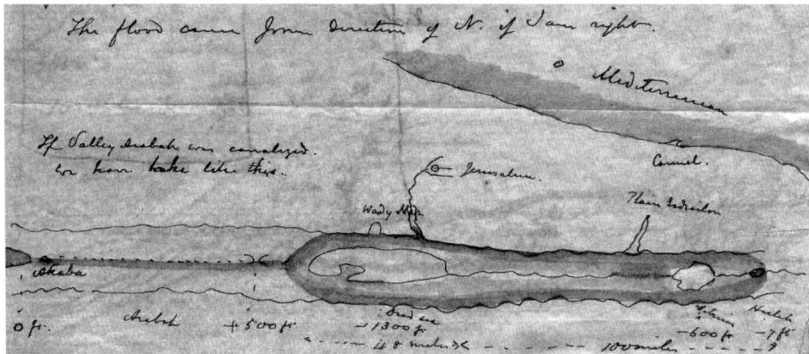

The Valley Arabah was canalized. We have lake like this.

---

[70] Sir Howard Elphinstone 1829 – 1890, was a close friend of Gordon and of Sir John Cowell.

Sir J Cowell KCB,   Jerusalem

Windsor   **20. 3. 83**

My dear Cowell,

Sorry to bother you, but I must substitute another arrangement of walls taken from Warren's Book 'Temple and Tomb'[71], which I only noticed yesterday. It differs from Warren only in bringing site of Holy Sepulchre into the area of the second wall. He puts it outside being bothered, I think with the "Camp of Assyrians" and with Agrippa's Wall. I keep to the site of Golgotha being the skull and the point of attack of Titus. He, Titus, had a Legion on Mt Olives, and there with him. I do not think he would have so separated them as to put his Legions to the West and one on the East.

Yours sincerely,

C G Gordon

PS I am having some models made of the Cup in olive wood and that of the" Rock" in stone.

El Kas The Cup

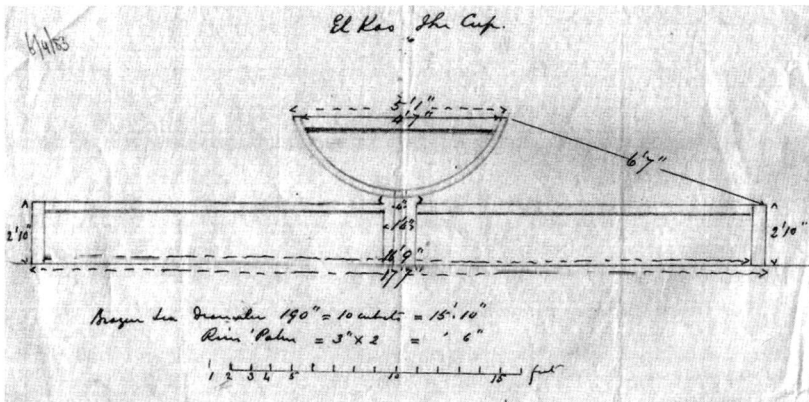

---

[71] Captain Charles Warren, RE, a British officer who conducted excavations in Jerusalem in 1867, including "Warren's Shaft"

Jerusalem

27. 4. 83

My dear Cowell,

I cannot write a long letter this time but just write a few lines to thank you for your last and to send you the sketch of a Baptistery, only two days ago opened out at Latrun[72], which if its distance did not object, according to the gospel, viz 10 stadia, would be Emmaus. The church they have opened out is wonderful as it is of Constantine's time. Huge stones equal to the Temple stones 7 to 8 feet long. Close to the big church is a Baptistery. It is the French clergy who are opening it out, a M.[73] St Croix, or some such name. You know the Franciscan Spanish monks have their Emmaus at Kobeieh[74] near Mispah. There will be a regular row about it. Latrun agrees in every way with Jerome's account of Emmaus, only it lacks in agreeing about 10 stadia, it has the three Roman roads and critics say if Jerome description is right, then distance is wrong, if distance is right, then no place agrees with Jerome's description. The so called Zion Hill is to me by the Scripture,

The Gibeon of Joshua,

Gibeon of the Levite

Gibeon of Saul

Nob of Doeg[75] also

Gibeon of the Tabernacle 'ere the Temple was built when it was separated from the Ark.

If ones goes by Scripture, I cannot see how it can be avoided to recognise it hitherto now. I do not put any great faith in the P EX F[76] they say a thing & stick to it and then try to fit in others, so they go from error to error. Another

---

[72] A site now called Emmaus-Nicopolis
[73] Her name was "Ms." (, Mademoiselle) de Saint-Cricq",
who paid, as a rich Donor, for the ruins of Amwas (Emmaus-Nicopolis), to be given to Nuns, early in 1875.
[74] Qubeiba today
[75] 1 Samuel, 21
[76] Palestine Exploration Fund

thing confuses is that Bible writers of notes and commentaries taken up with false sites and expedite on them, which perpetuates error. A clergyman here, Rev'd Claughton, was quite shocked when I doubted the so-called Zion and its Coenaculum[77] which I believe is tombs of Kish[78] and Saul. The Holy Hill is the figure of which the skull is the head. All the evil comes from the West, Saul's city. I hope that you and Lady Cowell are well and family and the Bladons are well.

Alex of Bulgaria[79] and Battenburg is at Jerusalem. Today is Greek Good Friday, lots of Russians with him. I do not go to Jerusalem except for a particular print. I do not care for sites, if I have the map.

Believe me, my dear Cowell

Yours sincerely,

C G Gordon

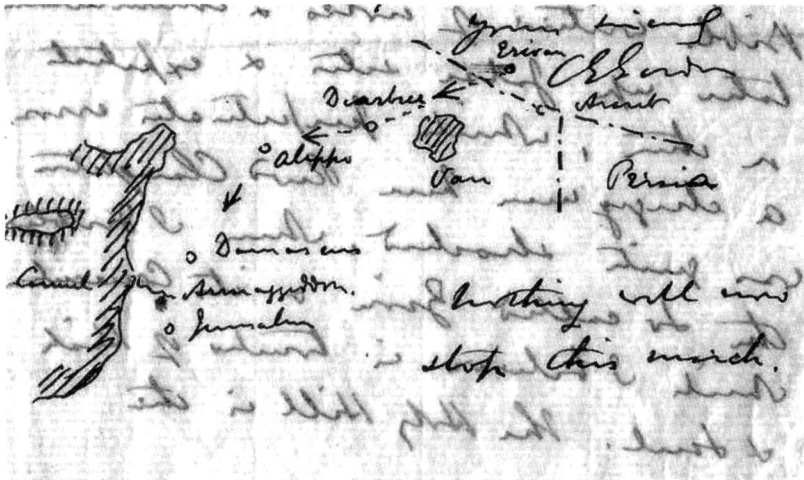

Nothing will now stop this march

---

[77] Possible site of 'The Last Supper' from 'cena' = supper (Latin).
[78] Father of Saul, first King of Israel
[79] Alexander Joseph of Battenberg GCB (5 April 1857 – 23 October 1893) was the first prince (knyaz) of modern Bulgaria, reigning from 29 April 1879 to 7 September 1886.

1. Gibeon of Joshua is West Hill Jerusalem. is Nob. is place
of rest Tabernacle from Saul till Solomon.

Jos. IX. & X. 4. Admazidon Come up to [...] & help [...]

2 Sam. XXI. 1.	2 Sam. VI. 3.	1 Ch. IX. 3
1 Sam. XVIII. 54	1 Ch. XV. 13	" " 19
1 Sam. XXI. 1.	" XVI. 5 = 2	" " 21
1 Sam. XIV. 16	" XXVI. 4. 2	" " 28
1 Samuel XIV. 3.	" XXXI = 15	" " 27
Isaiah X. 32	" VI. 32. 39	" " 32
		" " 34
		" " 35
		" " 38

1 Chron. XVI. 1 - 39	1 Kings IX. 1
" " 29	1 Sam. XV. 25
1 Kings I. 39	1 Ch. XIII. 3
1 " I. 50	1 Ch. X. 14
1 " II. 28. 29	1 Sam. XXVIII. 6

2. Gibeon of Levit.

Jud. XIX. 9.

Joseph. Ant. V. 11. V. 11. 8 Market place Upper market
Joseph [...] [...] Place
Judges XX

3 Gibeah of Saul 1 Sam. IX & XXXX

1 Ch. VIII. 29. 33

1 Ch. IX. 35

2 Sam XXI. 14

1 Sam IX. 8. unto Nagid Philistine [...]

1 Sam XI. 4

1 Sam XIII. 2 Gibeah of Benjamin & Nagib. [...]

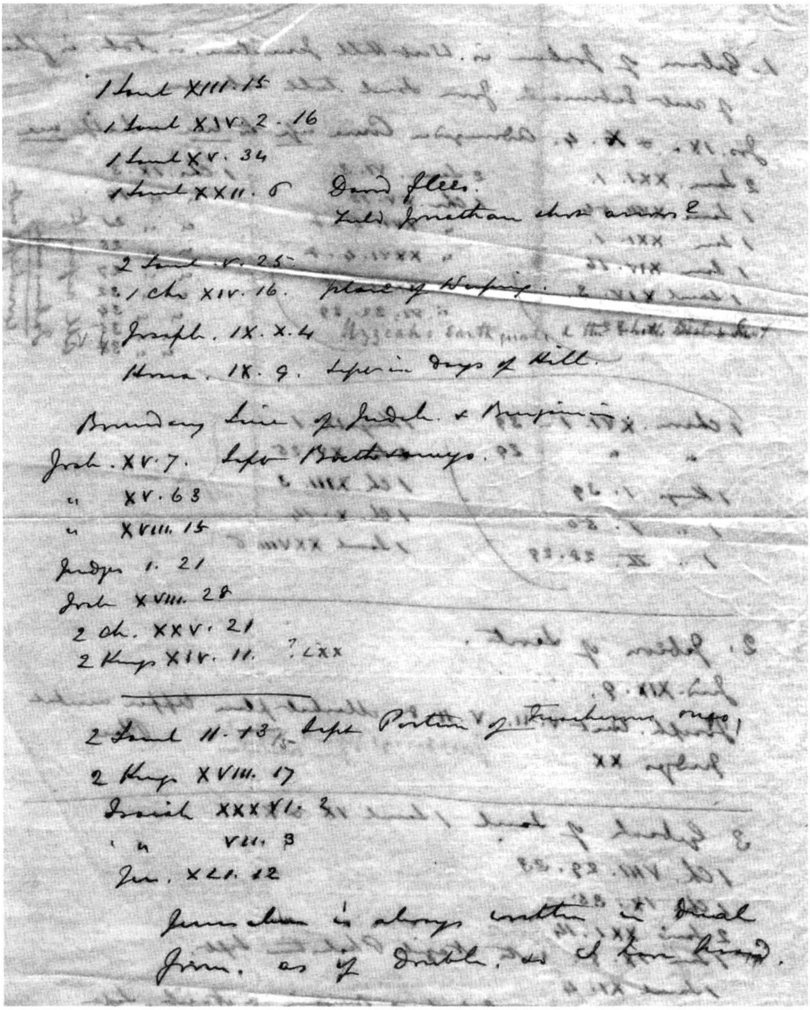

1 Sam. XIII. 15
1 Sam. XIV. 2. 16
1 Sam. XV. 34
1 Sam. XXII. 5   David flees.

2 Sam. ? 25
1 Chr. XIV. 16.   place of Worship.
Joseph. IX. X. 4
Home. IX. 9.

Boundary line of Judah & Benjamin
Josh. XV. 7.   before Bethsemes.
   "   XV. 63
   "   XVIII. 15
Judges 1. 21
Josh. XVIII. 28
2 Ch. XXV. 21
2 Kings XIV. 11.   ? LXX

2 Sam. 11. 13,   before Portion
2 Kings XVIII. 17
Isaiah XXXVI.
   "   VII. 3
Jer. XLI. 12

Jerusalem is always written in dual
form, as of Double, as I have heard.

Jerusalem is always written in dual form, so I have heard

Jerusalem

7th May 83

My dear Cowell,

Thanks for your kind letter 19th April. It is a pleasure to me to know you are interested. Sorry my plans are not better done, but have many of them to do. I have got out a paper on the Western, or so called Zion Hill, being the Gibeon of Joshua, Gibeon of Levites, Gibeon of Saul, Nob, Gibeon of Tabernacle. Also that the boundaries of Judah & Benjamin and the Western Hill are from Zion Hill up Tyropoeon valley.

Nob,

Gibeon of Tabernacle.

Also that the boundarys of Judah and Benjamin cut the Western Hill from Zion Hill up to Tyropean Valley

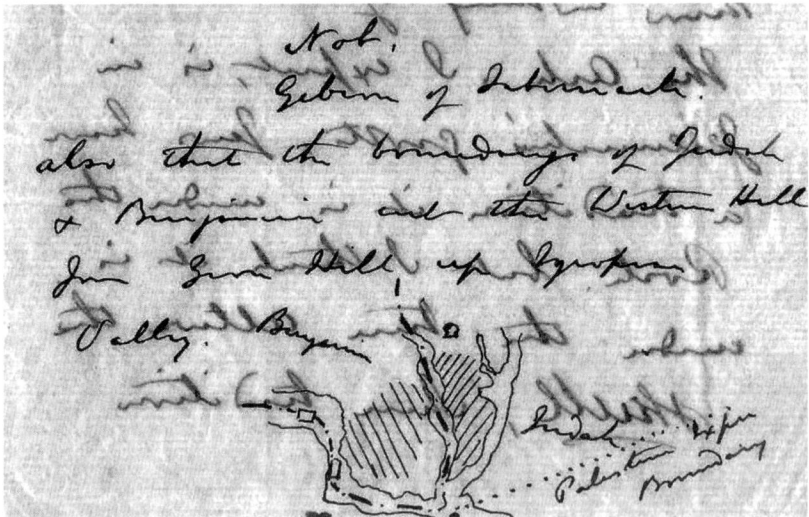

Strange that Palestine Explor.[80] Committee cut Judah out altogether from Jerusalem. I will send it to you when I have time to make a copy, for it is a long affair & and has given me a mint[81] of work to extract. What I say is that

---

[80] Palestine Exploration Fund
[81] Mint or mound?

Scripture does not go against these sites, as for Eusebius etc., etc., I know nothing of them.

The Ark, I suspect is in Jeremiah's grotto, Jews have a tradition it is under the Rock, but I think it is under the true Altar, the <u>Skull</u>, where tradition places Jeremiah's writing of Lamentations. The Ark will not be found by man. I think it will be brought out again at the second coming, for it appears in Heaven vide Revlns[82]. The Walls are a terribly dry subject but I will try & save you the bother in a few days and give you the reasons of my suppositions. Some are very curious. Josephus speaks of Womens Towers. Jeremiah of 'towers of funeraries'. If you took out Kainoinnus in Latin Fornex[83] you will see the argument. Herodias[84] was in that Citadel or Palace, & she was not a good woman, also look at Josiah breaking down the high places which Manasseh had made at Gate of Governor of City **2 Kings XXIII** & also mentioned by Nehemiah. All these little links connect the Jaffa Gate with the Women's Towers & Tower of Funeraries and also the shrine of grave of Nehemiah and grave of Josiah. Also the Dragon pool of Neh.[85] with the Mamilla Pool[86], or Serpent's Pool of present day & also there are some remarks which make me think this is the Potter's Field, the Fuller's field, the field of blood, Akeldama. I will go into all these for you when I have time.

I seldom go to bed before 10.30 pm and am up at daybreak early, and seldom, except Sundays, see anyone. Query, is this not selfish? I do not know exactly, I know I am mischievous if I go out much & talk about things I feel strongly about ie. Egypt, etc., not that I can[87] much now for not funding my thoughts in these things, they die in me. I have gone for the stars, these splendid nights & know them pretty fairly. I wish you had a clerk who, if I sent you papers could copy them, for you. If I have so many copies to make and I do hate the copying work. Really the Gibeon paper is splendid, & took a lot of time. Do not trouble to write a long letter, just scribble the points you disagree with in half margin and I will send it back. Joab met Abner at upper pool, Serpent's Pool, he killed Amasa near Montefiore's Cottages.[88]

---

[82] Revelation
[83] i.e. Latin script
[84] Herodias (queen of Galilee), was the wife of Herod Antipas, who was tetrarch (ruler appointed by Rome) of Galilee, in northern Palestine, from 4 BC to AD39. She had John the Baptist killed according to Mark 6 and was formerly the wife of Philip the Tetrach, brother of Herod Antipas by whom she had Herodias.
[85] Nehemiah
[86] Mamilla Pool, situated on west side of Jerusalem, now in Independence Park
[87] Possibly missing 'do'
[88] A Jewish philanthropist, Sir Moses Montefiore built homes and a windmill for workers here from 1860, called Mishenot Shaanaim today

I have gone into the anointing of Solomon and Adonijah.

One cannot agree yet to have Manasseh's well in front of Jaffa Gate, for Nehemiah will have 1000 cubits between the Valley Gate and Dung Gate, that is my reason. I wish I could sketch the front, for I find no notion when the well outside the 1000 cubit wall was made. It must have been made after Nehemiah, unless one changes the Valley Gate, near Dragon or Serpent's Pool.

I expect that the waters will come, as tradition says from Damascus Gate, from the true Altar the Skull, must split through the ridge near Montefiore's cottages & reach the Valley of Giants[89] El Burkieh[90], to reach the Mediterranean Sea.

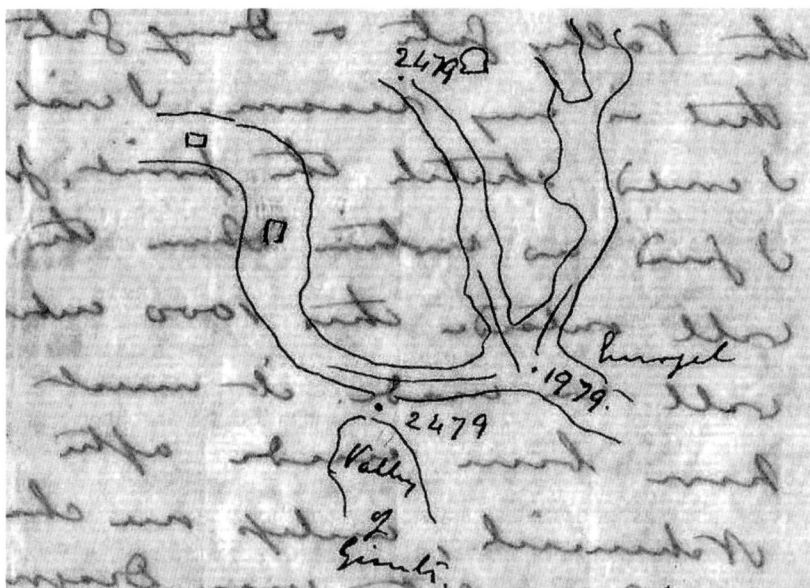

Valley of Giants   En Rogel

My brother Henry has two papers on the flood & on the 4 Rivers. Ask him by a P. card to send them to you.

---

[89] This is today's Emek Rafaim – same Biblical meaning "Valley of Giants"
[90] El Burqueiah today

Several passages in **Proverbs, Job** etc. allude to the giants who perished in the Flood, groaning under the crust of earth. **Canticles IV.4**[91] has "thy neck is like the Tower of David, builded for an Armoury." **Nehemiah III (20)** mentions the Armoury. I think Nehemiah's sepulchres of kings means those Kings buried in garden that Josephus mentions at the Cotton quarries where they say David and other kings were buried, oddly enough about 10 or 12 American & English gentlemen & ladies live just over the wall at Cotton Garth[92], they believe that our Lord has come and that He is with them in secret. They do not know my theory, they are very charitable. The Coenaculum[93] is Kish and Saul's sepulchre is the place of superstition and kissing stones. It is right it should be a false site.

Kindest regards to Du Plat, he is daily in my memory at 7 AM.

Kindest regards to Lady Cowell & your family & Mrs Cowell. I am very sorry that Her Majesty is suffering from that strain. What a good Queen she has been to us.

Believe me

Yours sincerely

C G Gordon

---

[91] Song of Songs

[92] Location is probably Mugharat al Kutan, the site of Zedekiah's Cave or Solomon's Quarry, beneath the Spafford Children's Centre, home to the early members of the American Colony on the old Walls, where Gordon later became a frequent visitor. They believed in the imminent Second Coming of the Messiah.

[93] On what is called today Mount Zion

My dear Cowell,

I send you a tracing of the division of the tribes. I imagine you have the Palestine map from which the tracing is taken. There will also come to you a model of the Rock & of the Laver or El Kas.

There still a very strong idea that Constantine's Basilica is still to be found under Skull Hill near that St Stephen's Church outside Damascus Gate. The French Consul, an old friend of mine, Langlais, who died a fortnight ago very suddenly, told me he hoped to get the money for the purchase of the Slaughter House & ground, but I could see plainly, he would have he lived, not been over inclined to open out the land, had it been seen it was likely to invalidate the present Holy Sepulchre. He was writing a dispatch, felt ill, was dead in five minutes. I believe we have no more consciousness or pain in death than we had in birth, it is only apparent.

I went to Jaffa, the other day, they have carefully walled up the Baptistery at Latrun[94] & and hid it from vulgar gaze. At Ramleh is the room Napoleon was in, at time of his invasion, he did not go to Jerusalem, for the Turks shut up the Xians[95] in the Holy Sepulchre & said they would massacre them, if he came, but I do not think it would stop him, it was to him a place of no interest apparently. The unique Mameluke[96] who escaped from Mehemet Ali's little Dinner party in Cairo citadel, died at Ramleh.

The man in all England who would give the best opinion on sacred sites if he would only judge by his knowledge of Scripture is Bishop Wordsworth of Lincoln[97]. He would know in a moment all allusions to the furnaces, fullers' field, etc., etc. What I find wearisome is the writing out so often of the same thing, otherwise I would write to him. I will write again soon. Kind regards to Lady Cowell, yourself and family.

Yours sincerely

C G Gordon

---

[94] Or Emmaus - Nicopolis, Byzantine Church Baptistry
[95] Christians
[96] A foreign soldier in the Ottoman Empire
[97] Bishop Christopher Wordsworth, (1807 – 1885) nephew of poet, Wordsworth, Bishop of Lincoln, 1869 -1885

Plan of Baptistry at Latrun

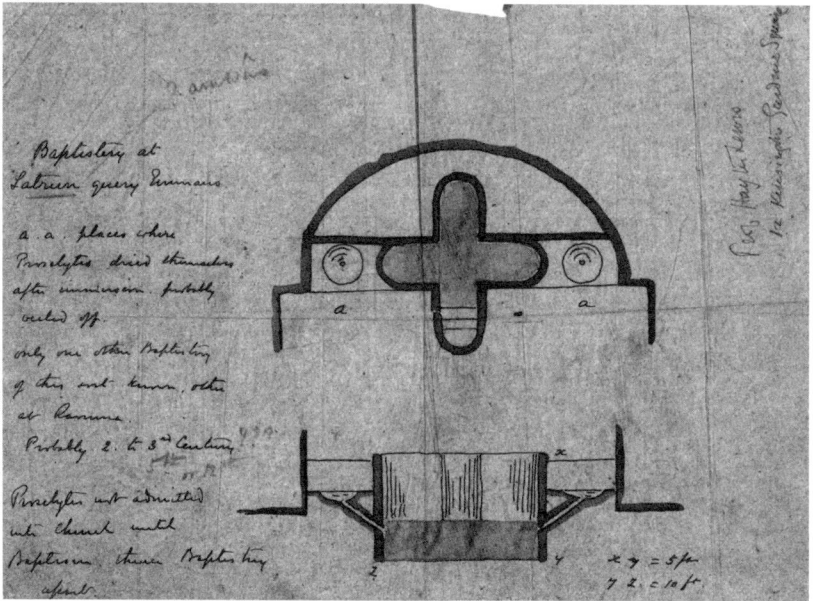

Baptistery at
Latrun query Emmaus

a & a Places where Proselytes dried themselves after immersion, probably
veiled off.

Only one other Baptistery of this known, other at Ravenna. Probably 2nd to
3rd Century

Proselytes not admitted to church until Baptism thence Baptistery apart

LETTERS AND NOTES
TO ACCOMPANY LETTERS WITHOUT DATES

Following goes with the letter of 8 3 83
MEMOS ON WALLS OF JERUSALEM

1. Herod attacked Jerusalem and took <u>first wall</u> in 40 days. <u>Second wall</u> in 15 days. In last attack some of the northern cloisters of Temple were burnt, which shows 2nd wall abutted on the Cloisters[98] of Temple and therefore must have been the line of defence of Antonia (Ant XIV xvi 2[99] for the above, Josephus) it also adds that the Jews retired into the inner court of the temple and the upper city, which fixes the upper city to be one where Citadel is.

2. Josephus on the Walls

(a) It is quite impossible to reconcile his statements about the number of towers in each wall, and their size and distance apart with the 33 furlongs circumference of city. (Wars V. iv. 3[100]) he says

Ist wall   90 towers 20 cubits square
2nd wall   40 towers   "   "
3rd wall   <u>60</u> towers   "   "
        190   "   = 3800 cubits at intervals of 200 cubits
                                        would be 20900 yards,

Which 33 furlongs are 5775 yards? Neither do I take any note of when Josephus mentions monuments which are definitely not known to be true sites. The Tyropoeon Valley is Gihon, & its upper pool is Josephus' Serpent Pool between which & city Titus levelled the ground (Wars V. iii, 2) & over which part are Herod's Monuments.

3. Josephus V iv 2[101] describes Walls thus:

"The Old Wall", strengthened by David and other Kings extends *"began on the north from Tower Hippicus, thence to Xistus, then to West Cloister of Temple."*

---

[98]

[99] Antiquities of the Jews XVI, xvi, 2 by Josephus
[100] Wars of the Jews by Josephus
[101] Wars of the Jews

It is evidently the wall running along the proper right hand of the Tyropoeon Valley and cropping it, to the Temple area, at about the same distance from S. West Angle as the Golden Gate is from the SE angle. This is the proper <u>third</u> wall. *"Which is the first or old wall, and it goes to Antonia."* I expect along the line of the conduit from Jeremiah's grotto. *"The third wall begins at Tower Hippicus as far as North quarter of city and Tower Psephinus, and bent again at turn of the corner, and joined old wall at Valley of Kedron.* This wall is the outer wall so I call it the first wall.

V iv 3[102] *"Tower Psephinus is at NW Corner , over against it is Tower Hipppicus and two others in <u>old Wall</u>. Phaselus and Mariamne[103]. Simon commands Upper city and old wall. John and Eleazar command in Temple, Antonia and Ophel"*

V viii 3[104] after capture of 2nd Wall, *"Simon fortifies his part as far as that gate, whence water is brought into Tower Hippicus,"* query is that gate not the Gennath Gate, is not water alluded to , the water of the conduit of Jeremiah's grotto?

V vii 4[105] *Titus attacks middle tower of 2nd wall. Castor, a Jew leaps into vault below,* can that vault be the conduit, which the line of wall must have nearly followed?

V viii. 1[106] mentions that the narrow streets lead obliquely to 2nd Wall which they do

Of 2nd Wall runs as shown

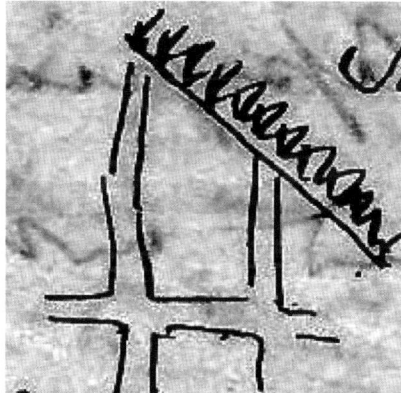

V vii 3[107] After capture of Hippicus *"Titus pitched camp in the place which was called the Camp of Assyrians within the city."* Josephus says: it <u>was called so</u> & was <u>within</u> the city and that does not imply that the Assyrian camp of siege was there for it was <u>within the city.</u> **Jeremiah** LII says Zedekiah rebels and Nebuchadnezzar come on 10th day 10th month of 9th year of Reign. City

---

[102] A Wars of the Jews by Flavius Josephus
[103] Phasaelus, a friend, and Mariamne, favourite wife, of Herod the Great
[104] Wars of the Jews
[105] Wars of the Jews
[106] Wars of the Jews
[107] Wars of the Jews

besieged till 9th day, 4th month of 11th year of his reign when it is captured, then a month after, comes Nebuchadnezzar & burnt the Temple and city & etc and it is this last date 10 5th month 11th year of Zedekiah which Jews keep as the fast of destruction of Jerusalem. I think that Nebuzaradan[108] camped at the "Camp of Assyrians" while he was engaged in this work and where there was no fighting. Hitherto this mention of Titus camping on place of camp of Assyrians during siege, which it became and could not be, for it was within the city.

V vi 1[109] "Acra no other than the Lower City".

V vi 2[110] could imply that Agrippa's wall to be the enlargement of the city on North taking in hill which is number four, Bethesda, vide plan. The moon shaped hill V vi 1[111] I expect is the hill just south of the Skull Hill Jeremiah's grotto.

The events of the siege are thus.

NB. The Tomb of the Kings are evidently not found.
Query they may be in Jeremiah's Grotto.

---

[108] Jeremiah 52:1 Captain of the King Nebuchadnezzar's Bodyguard.
[109] Wars of the Jews
[110] Wars of the Jews
[111] Wars of the Jews

PS. Josephus VI VIII. 4 end of Paragraph tends to show that the Tower of Hippicus was not taken in the attack 15th April of 1st Wall, so Hippicus must not be where I put it, Pserpinus, Josephus does not mention

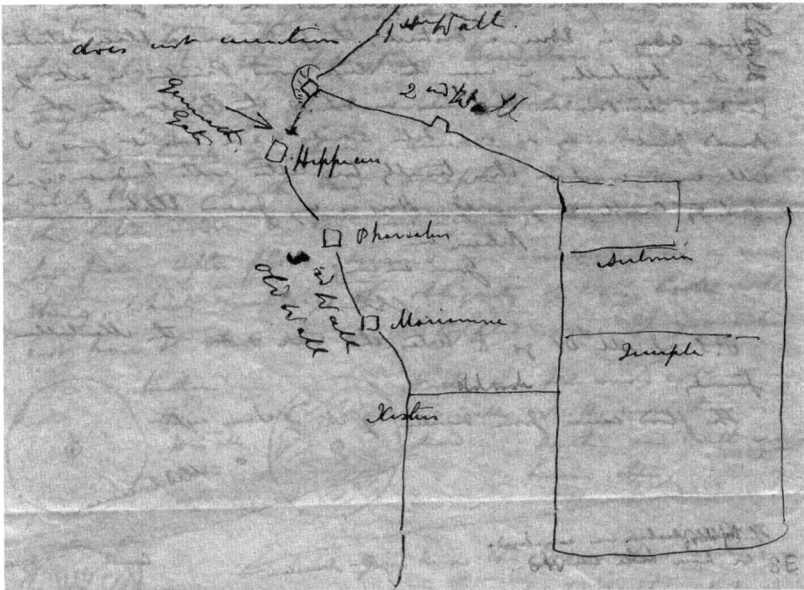

SITE OF TEMPLE

1. Herod was not inspired in his building the Temple; Solomon was, for David gave him instructions, based on what he had by the Spirit. **I Chronicles 28:12**

2. Width of present Kubbet, or Dome of Rock is just the width of the Outer Court of Solomon's Temple.

3. The Veil of H. Of Holies hung over 11th step going up to Rock each step being 2 cubits. Length of flight of steps 50 cubits, 25 steps the Ark rested on edge of 6th step thus

Daniel says 'trodden down shall be the Sanctuary' Daniel VIII. 13.

4. The Temple was double the tabernacle except for the Altar. The Tabernacle altar was 3 cubits high, that of the Temple 10 cubits high. The Altar of the Tabernacle was ¼ of altar temple except in height. Why 10 cubits and not 12 for Temple altar because rock gave the additional 2 cubits thus:

5. Brazen Sea "to be right side of last end over against the South." He set the Sea to the right side of house eastward against the south. 2 Chronicles IV and I Kings VIII. Jews wail at wall opposite cup or Brazen Sea. Entry into Jewish church by laver, entry into Christ has church by the rite of Baptism. Jews would never pray towards H. of Holies or wish to enter there before they wash at the Laver and then would go to altar. They wail for purification by Baptism.

6. ? missing or misnumbered

7. Herod's Temple had no Ark. Jeremiah had it, perhaps in his grotto near Damascus Gate.

8. Only the Altar and Laver c. & the Rock are left. They are the two sacraments of the Christian Church. When the Crusaders held Jerusalem they had their Altar on the Rock.

9. The Cup is 10 cubits in diameter same as Brazen Sea. I will send details of the Rock and the Cup.

MORE NOTES ON GOLGOTHA

Golgotha on Hill was Jeremiah's Grotto.

1. This hill is outside gates near city where many roads pass.

2. From long time back the Slaughter House of City has been there.

3. It is N. of City. Shew Bread table is in it. The Cross was the Tree of Life. Christ was born in S, will come in E, crucified in N. Titus took city not 300yds from this hill. The mounds are still visible.

4. People say that there was another outer wall enclosing this hill, but this outer wall was built by Herod Agrippa in AD 44, 12 years after crucifixion. Titus took city in AD 70, Josephus describes city of that epoch. Josephus' city is as on page.

Figure 1

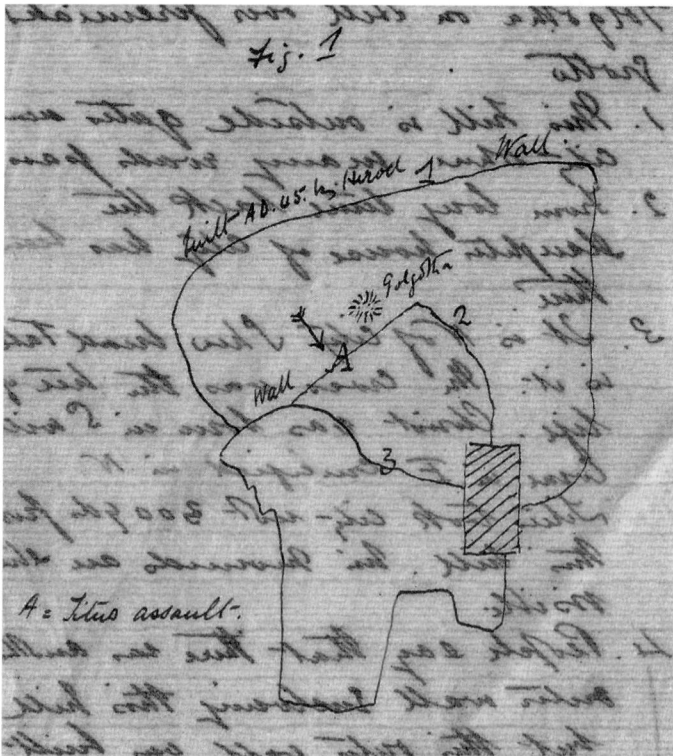

Figure 2

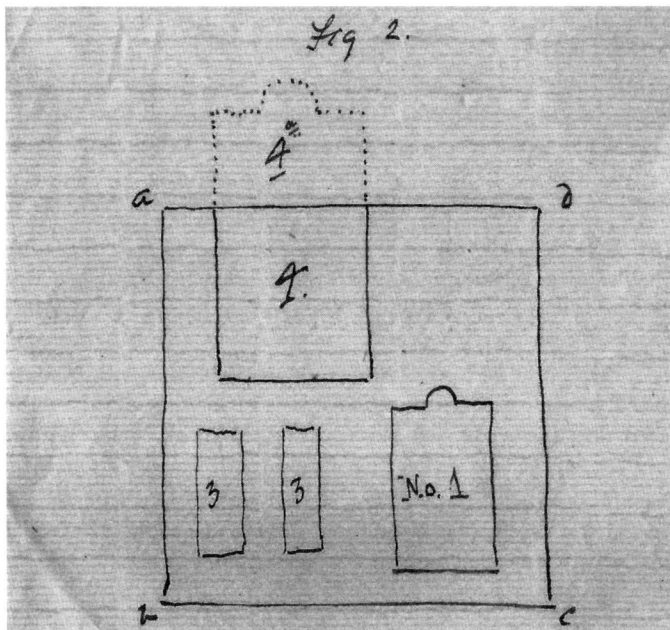

A SKETCH OF THE CHURCHES ON THE SITE OF
THE POSSIBLE MARTYDOM OF ST STEPHEN

5. In sketch to the left of the hill Jeremiah's grotto is a place (fig 2) coloured yellow, this has been bought by the French lately[112]. There was a large heap of cinders there, a man bought it to build upon the mound and found the site of a Church No 1 and two large cisterns. Nos. 3 & 3. The French gave £2000 for plot, on expectations they opened out 4 and found foundations of much larger church but the W. end the altar was out of the land and the man who owns the land wants £7000 for it. I have done what I can in Paris to get D'Avril, an old friend of mine to buy it, for otherwise some other community will buy it and make a church as they have the <u>altar</u> of the church of 4th century. What these ruins are, no one knows as yet, but they think it is St Stephen's Church; an Empress[113] built a huge church in memory of Stephen the Martyr outside the Gate. The Persians destroyed it in 600AD[114] and Crusaders in

---

[112] St Stephen's Church or St Etienne, at the Ecole Biblique

[113] Empress Eudocia, wife of Theodosius II, visited Jerusalem in 438 AD, and dedicated the building on May 15th, 439 built by Juvenal, Bishop of Jerusalem, she paid for enlarging and embellishing it and was buried here in 460

[114] Probably 614 AD

11th Century found the site and not having sufficient money to rebuild the Empress's church they built a small one on it. So that church No.1 is the Crusaders' church and Church 4 is the Empress Church. I say the cisterns are the cisterns for water separation. Numbers XIX and the old place of Jerusalem is thus. This is in Smith's Bible Dictionary and I consider the sketch at N. is the church just found, if so then the gate Damascus is Stephens Gate and not the Gate called Stephen's[115], near the Pool of Bethesda on Cedron's[116] side. Now the point of all this is why did the Empress build her church to Stephen outside Gate, unless it was because Stephen was stoned there? You can see by the map of 12th Century Crusaders were not struck by this for they show Golgotha inside city. Yet why did Empress put it outside unless Stephen was stoned there – and if Stephen was stoned there so soon after our Lord's crucifixion? It is more than probable that he was stoned in the same place of execution as our Lord was crucified on. The change of name to the gate near the Pool Bethesda, can be accounted for the Catholic clergy fearing the authenticity of the present Holy Sepulchre being disputed – for there is no doubt but that the Christian laity, who on the strength of the clergy's statement that the site of the crucifixion was at the place now occupied by the Holy Sepulchre, came and worshipped there for years, will not be pleased to find the clergy lied. It is a just punishment for superstition, one can imagine what a fearful row will take place if Jeremiah's hill is the true Golgotha.

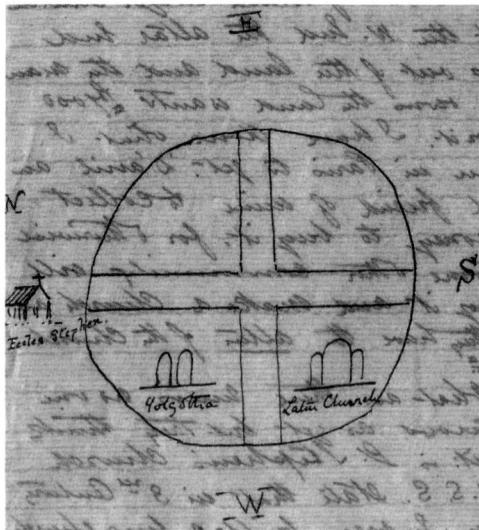

---

[115] Or now called Lion Gate.
[116] Or Kidron

ZECHARIAH ON OUTFLOW OF WATERS

Septuagint, **Zechariah XIV 5 – 10** does not agree with A.V.[117] in the upheaval of the land near Jerusalem. It says the valley shall be closed up, verse 5.

Allusion is made to the earthquake during the time King Uzziah, read Josephus, Bk I X, Ch XI , 4[118], as to the blocking of the Kidron valley at En Rogel, is the earthquake, which was a type of the coming earthquake when Mt Olives splits in two, one half to the N, one half to the South.

NB I am rather inclined to analyse the traditions of Damascus Gate, to think the outflow of waters will be from the ROCK, of Haram, the old Levitical Altar, not the gospel Altar of the Skull, (the water ought to come from that part of the figure, scratch this out) out of his belly will flow living waters.

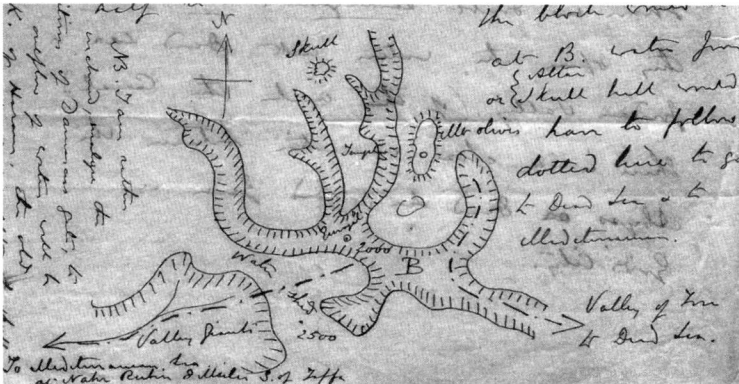

Azal means 'Root' or 'extremity'[119] of Mountain, I expect it is same as Stone Ezel where Jonathan and David met. Oddly enough near this is the Perets or Breech of Uzzah, who touched the Ark and Peretz Bowl where David made Breach, Breach of Waters **2 Samuel V, 20** of Philistines in Valley of Rephaim or Giants.

There is no doubt earthquakes will happen when they open the waters into Dead Sea & Jordan Valley (if they make the Canal). There is a close connection between the Abyss or Dead Sea and Zion, or God's City.

---

[117] King James Authorised Version – printed in English in 1611
[118] Antiquities of the Jews X, x, 4 incorrectly referenced in text.
[119] Word unclear, dictionaries suggest extremity or proximity

This part could come from another letter without a salutation

I like it in a way, and expect it, it is God's portion even to wish for holiness apart from Him, is evil, for it is wished for , because the flesh will glory, Schapara (not the forger[120]), was grumbling about his troubles, his lamb aged 5 inter this "Oh! Happy! How you can talk so! <u>You know</u> you can tell Jesus all about it & He will help you."

In reference for "help" see *Gesenius DCXIX Ingellis Edition*

As for Neby Samwil[121], according to P. Ex F.[122] found papers the date of its name is only 300 yrs. old and is from an Arab sheikh. It is 4 miles from Jerusalem, and not on any great road.

If you look at the papers on Gibeon, you will see, I put Solomon's Gibeon on the west Hill. Unless it is a great bore read those papers again: you will see I put the Mizpah of Gedaliah **Jer. XLI** at the Mizpah of Samuel. 2 …. II[123], over against Jerusalem. I quite have left it out in my view. I send you another sketch of the Hills of Jerusalem. You cannot mistake The Cistern under Jeremiah's grotto is exceedingly deep, but I do not know if there is an exit from it or an ingress into it from one side, I have asked my friend Schick[124] to find out. I have no doubt that it fed the Schick conduit, the oesophagus.

I think that the crop stood on top of the skull in centre of it not where the Slaughter House is for Titus would never had put his tent under the brow of a hill, to be under cover. Did you ever look up the word 'side' πλαγίον, Leviticus 1. II - Hebrew has "yarek" thigh.

I will conclude, for the moment, Tower of Ramleh must wait a bit.

With kindest regards to you all & Mrs Freeman,

Believe me,

Yours sincerely

CG Gordon

PS You have a sketch which shows where I have put Mizpeh and Eben-ezer.

---

[120] Shapira
[121] Traditional burial place of the Prophet Samuel
[122] Palestine Exploration Fund, founded in 1865 to conduct surveys of the topography of the Holy Land
[123] Undeciferable
[124] Conrad Schick, archaeologist, city planner and architect in Jerusalem at this time, died 1901, he made a plan of Jeremiah's Grotto

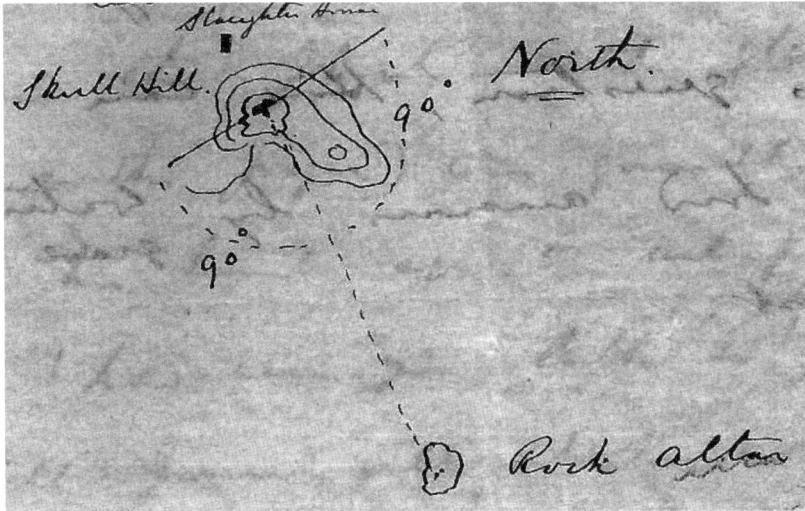

Rock Altar

East Hill of Zion Resembling Human Form

Ephesians I:22.23

Gave Him to be head to the church, which is His <u>body</u>. Therefore the Body of Christ is His Church, and the members of churches are members of <u>His Body,</u> flesh of His flesh, bone of His bone. There is no doubt, (I believe, humbly) that the many scriptures on this subject regard literally Christ as a <u>Head</u>, church as a <u>body,</u> one Christ, who is Lord of Heaven and earth. However glorified that our Christ may be, it is assuredly a man, a human figure, made up of many members, filled with one spirit. Because the Head is Divine the members are partakers of Divine nature.

I think Gal. IV 25 and 26[125] show the Jerusalem which is <u>above</u> is typical of the Jerusalem below, both are churches. One triumphant one militant, they correspond to the church on earth & church In heaven, they correspond to saints on earth, & saints in heaven, man on earth, and man in heaven.

We have seen that the church above not yet complete, not yet perfected, will be, when perfected the Body of Christ. His glorified body. The body of Christ the Church is <u>one</u> (double underline), part of its numbers have risen part are on earth, both parts those risen and those on earth are members of one glorified

---

[125] Galatians

52

body the Church of Christ. Those on earth are in bondage, those above are free. Christ when on earth was in bondage. He is now glorified, so far for the Head when on earth He was same Man, as He is now, except that He is glorified, as He is, so are His members, when the members of the church in bondage join the other members of the free church above they are not changed, they are glorified.

From this, I deduce that the typical city Zion, of the church on earth should resemble the prototype Zion of the church above, which is in form of man and thence I infer that the figure of the East Hill is not a fanciful one, there are many, many, passages which cause the deduction that things seen as copies of things unseen and before I ever came to this country, I felt instinctively that what I have seen as to human figure, would be the case. If the Temple itself was a copy of the Temple in Heaven, then so must its surroundings be. Hebrews distinctly points out that the temple of Zion was copy of God's dwelling place. IX. 24 **(Hebrews)**, so was the Tabernacle. God's dwelling place is Christ who is one with His body the Church.

I have not time to go into detail of the similarity of the human body to tabernacle & Temple, but to me, it is perfect, even to the 9 months it took to make, its wonders of being made, the quickening & its birth, and I feel instinctively, that if I knew Hebrew, I should find some words used for setting up tabernacle & for birth, indeed children are teknon. Hebrews XI.10 God in the teknites, Christ is the Carpenter, teknon of universe, though they did not mean it. Eve was builded out of the rib.

Members of Christ are stones living of temple. This Church or body of Christ is the House made without hands.

All shows forth the indwelling of God in man. The Head has risen, & on His ascension, He sent the Holy Ghost to live in us, thus it is we have no Holy of Holies in our churches, the Holy of Holies is in us.

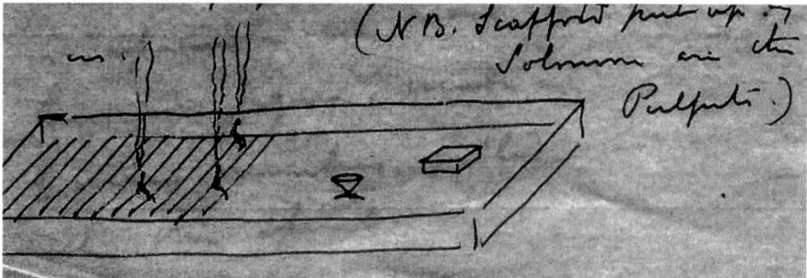

Scaffold put up by Solomon are the Pulpits

The word used to set up, to rear up the Tabernacle is "qum"[126], to bring forth children is "tikto"[127]

The raison d'etre of the Tabernacle was to guard the 10 words of God in the Ark, the covenant, the seed of God, the Rock that begat thee, that He might dwell among them, make Me a Sanctuary.

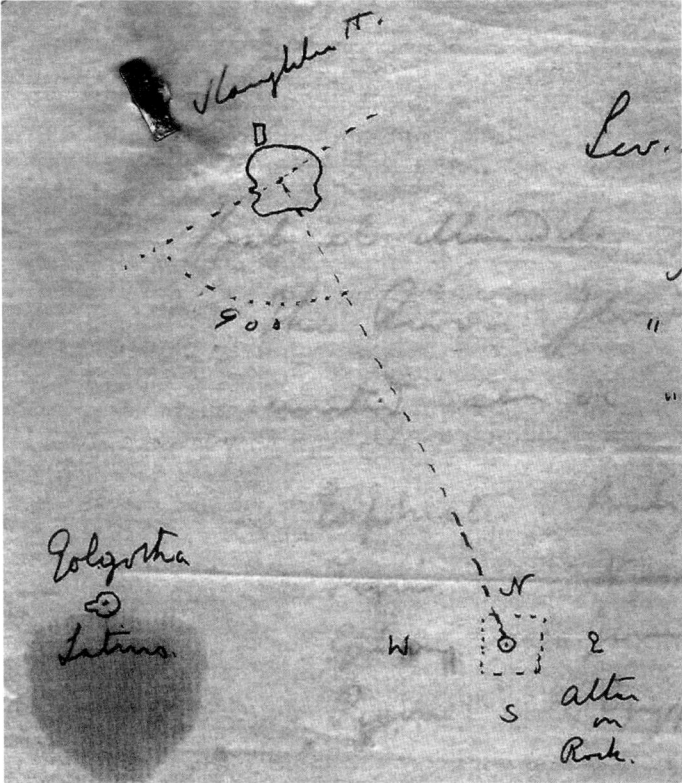

Golgotha   **Slaughter House above**   **Altar on Rock**

Latins

Leviticus 1.11

Slay victims on the side of Altar Northwards, read "slay victims slantwise to Altar Northwards." πλαγίον

---

[126] Arabic & Hebrew for "raise up"
[127] Greek

If Cross placed thus, whole city & Mt Olives embraced by stretched out arms. *"All the day long have I stretched out my hands."*

Here at Skull Hill, close the Slaughter House of Jerusalem was Titus 1 to 2m. The Roman Eagle took the heart of Zion by throat, for close there was the breach. Jeremiah wrote Lamentations in the cave. The Ark of Covenant is there. There is the true altar out of which will flow Ezekiel's Rivers, the Gihon will burst forth. The West hill is busier than ever, the East Hill is a field almost.

All dimensions of altar tabernacle quadrupled except height, viz:

Altar Inc 5 x 5 x 3

Altar Temple 20 x 20 x 10 why not 12 squared because altar is in Rock

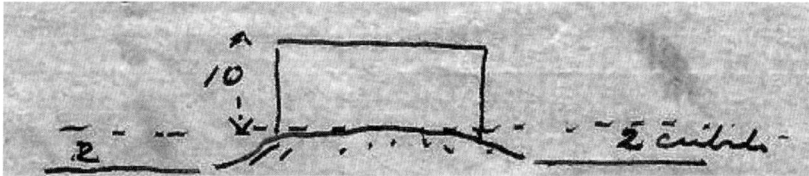

Bab el Mandel: Gate of World

The Rivers flowed down from their heads and untied at or near Seychelles.

Euphrates   Babylon 4

Tigris   Nineveh 3   all connected with Israel

Gihon   Jerusalem 2

Pison   Egypt 1

Trail goes first to No. 1, then to No 2, No 3, No 4.

All detail will be in papers with my brother. If ever you went to South'ton[128] to 5 Rockstone Place, you would see the forbidden fruit. The Breadfruit is the Tree of Life. Things are saved for a time. Ark was taken by Philistines. Titus carried off Candlesticks & Incense Altar, all most Holy to the Lord.

Later Holy Sepulchre, site of idolatry, on evil hill, west of altar, idolatry, adultery. Skull Hill deserted, on North slantwise to Altar.

Kuryat al Enab[129]

---

[128] Southampton, Gordon's sister's home
[129] Abu Ghosh today

Ramathaim Zophim

Kirjath Jearim   60 furlongs   Jerusalem

Armathaim

(Ramah and Gibeah High Place)

Arimathea

Emmaus

Ramathaim "Heights" dual

Aramathaim   "

Arimathea   "

Samuel when he anointed Saul was attending & sacrificing before Ark Covenant. Resting place of Ark. Resting place of the Lord abide with us. Joseph of Arimathea died at Glastonbury.

Zion is the church, the body of Christ, you have the Skull four times mentioned as Golgotha. If there is a skull there is also the body.

Zion beautiful for situation, joy of the earth, situated on sides of the north, situated on Ribs of N. same work as "pierced Him in rib." "Took a rib and builded woman." πλευρα The beloved of the Lord will rest in safety, the Lord will cover him, he shall rest between his shoulders. "Humerus", "Arms" Blessing Benjamin, Deuteronomy. Benjamin Hill is the bad Hill. Zion the good.

As for Gihon, it is a long story, which you must get from my brother.

Gihon is the Gihon of Eden

Pison is the Blue Nile

Euphrates

Tigris

The Garden of Eden was at or near Seychelles, and Eden is the district

THE WESTERN HILLS OF ZION

Gibeah, Gibeon etc.

This will only be a <u>sketch.</u> For details ask my brother for papers & sketches.

Judah & Benjamin both possessed a part if the area of Jerusalem, which was their frontier. All Bibles merely give Jerusalem to Benjamin the passages of A.V.[130]

Septuagint agree except in one place where AV (in pencil Joshua 18: 19) has En Shemesh. Sept., Beth Samys and the situation of this place is the question.

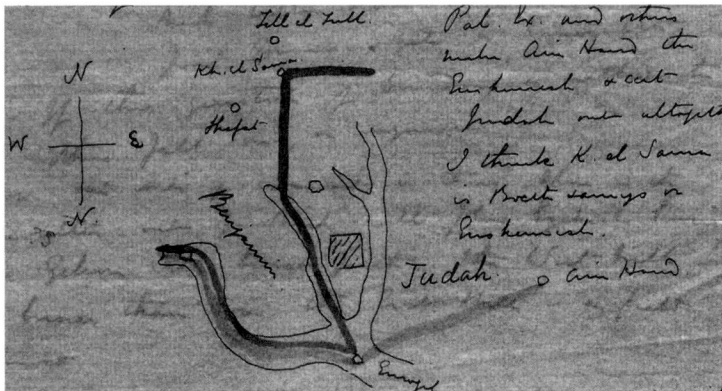

Pal. Ex. and others make Ain Harod the En Shemesh and cut Judah out altogether. I think K. el Sama[131] is: Beth Samys or En Shemesh.

Consequently I place frontier in red. Pal. Ex[132] place it in yellow.

1. It is impossible to deny Judah a part of Jerusalem.
2. Do that, if Judah possessed part, that part was Zion.
3. Ain Harod is an arbitrary position, & cuts Judah out altogether.
4. Kh. El Sama corresponds as Breth Samys and in in place where Amaziah was defeated by Jehoash, King of Israel which latter broke down wall 400 cubits from Damascus Gate to corner gate.

If this question of boundary is settled, the others fall in, in sequence.

---

[130] Authorised Version of King James Bible
[131] Khirbet es Sauma'a, just south of Tell el Ful, within Shu'fat, a northern suburb of Jerusalem
[132] Palestine Expedition Fund

PASSAGES ON POOLS & CONDUITS

Notes on Diagram: I expect this brook which runs through land was a conduit from El Bireh which Hezekiah banked and brought in by conduit.

Isaiah XXII 9. 10 King James Version

He gathered waters of Lower Pool. He also made ditch (A) between two walls (b & c) for water Old Pool. (d) he looked not to the Maker of it who fashioned it long ago.

Septuagint version

One had turned water of old Pool (d) into city. He poured water between the two walls (b, c) within the ancient pool (d) he looked not to Him who made it from the beginning regarded not Him who created it.

Isaiah VII 2 (3 in pencil) Met Ahaz at end of conduit of Upper Pool (d) in the highway of Fullers field. Septuagint. The Pool (d) upper way of Fullers field.

Nehemiah II. 13. Gate of Valley (e) even before Dragon[133] Wall (d) Septuagint to north of wall of Fig trees (?)

2 Chron.XXXIII 4. 30

Much people gathered together who stopped all fountains, and brook that ran thro' midst of land (Gihon) stopped upper water course (k) of Gihon and brought water (f) straight down West end of City of David.

Septuagint. Collected many people, stopped walls of water, and river that flowed through city (Gihon) stopped the course of water of Gihon, and brought water (f) down straight south? of city of David.

2 Kings XX 20

Made a pool a conduit, and brought water into city.

Septuagint Fountain and aqueduct and brought water into city.

Hezekiah's Wall, **2 Ch. XXXII** 5 The other wall without (op)

Mannaseh's Wall **2 Ch. XXXIII 14** Wall from west side of Gihon to Fish Gate (m, n)

Septuagint I do not understand here they appear to mix up repairs Ophel with this new wall.

Note in pencil: 34 years elapsed between Hezekiah and Manasseh.

See Josephus who explained in Antiquities X III 2 the double work of restoration and rebuilding.

THE POTTERS FIELD

Tregellus' Gesenius & Young's Annotated Concordance had for Jer. XIX. 2 *"Go into the valley of the Son of Hinnom which is at the entrance of East Gate"* unique use of the word Charsuth or Charisith (Septuagint has Chersith.) Both above consider the word ought to be Potters Gate, it opens to the Valley of Hinnom. Where there, he is to fight the battle, and say verse 6 *"this place shall be no more called Topeth or the Valley of 'son of Hinnom'. "*

All that can be said is that the Potters Gate opened on Valley of Hinnom, that in Valley of Hinnom the earthen bottle was broken as he Jeremiah went to the Potters House Jeremiah 18:1 it would seem that the Potters Gate, Potters House, Potters Field, Valley of Hinnom, Tophet were all in close proximity of one another.

---

[133] Jackal in NIV

Plan of Solomon's Temple

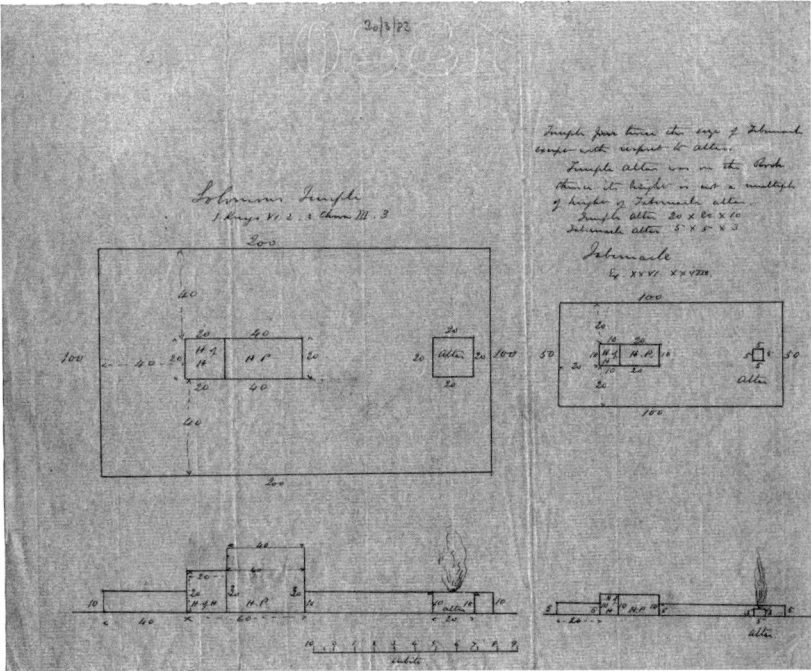

SOURCE MATERIAL

Elton, Lord, General Gordon, 1954, London, Collins.

Gordon, Charles, Letters to Sir John Pollock from Jerusalem, 1883, The Garden Tomb Archives

Gordon, Charles, Eden and Golgotha Palestine Exploration Fund Journal, April 1885

Nutting, Anthony, Gordon, Martyr and Misfit. World Books 1966

Pollock, John, Gordon, the Man behind the Legend. Oxford: Lion, 1993

Spafford, Bertha, Our Jerusalem, Jerusalem 1950

Whiston, William, The Works of Flavius Josephus, Antiquities of the Jews, Wars of the Jews

APPENDIX

Palestine Exploration Fund Article of April 1884 by Charles G. Gordon Eden and Golgotha

INDEX

SUBJECT	PAGE
Aden	29
Agrippa, King Herod A.ll	14, 30, 41, 43, 47
Ahaz, King	58
Ain (Ein) Harod	57
Akaba, Gulf of	25, 26, 27
Akeldama, Field of Blood	36
Altar or Table of the Lord	11, 12, 13, 15-18, 20, 21, 23, 36, 37, 45, 46, 50, 54, 55
Altar of Incense	55
Antonia Fortress, Tower	15
Arabah, Valley of	25-27, 29
Arimathea, Joseph of	56
Ark of the Covenant	10, 11, 14, 21, 22, 36, 45, 46, 50, 54, 55, 56
Assyrians, Camp of	21, 22, 42, 43
Bab el Mandel	25, 55
Babylon	26, 55
Battenburg, Prince Alex	32
Benjamin, tribe	35, 56, 57
Bethesda, Pool of	6, 43, 49
Beth Samys	57
Beth Shemesh	57
Bradons	5
Brazen Sea (Laver)	11, 12, 15, 46
Cambridge, Duke of	5
Cedron (Kidron)	49
Christ, Jesus	11, 18-24, 47, 52, 53, 56
City of David	59
Coenaculum	32
Cotton Quarries	38
Cotton Garth	38
Crusaders	6, 13, 48, 49
Claughton, Rev	32
Constantine, Emperor	10, 13, 31, 39
Damascus Gate	6, 7, 13, 14, 21, 24, 37, 57

D'Avril, Baron	48
David, King	14, 38
Dead Sea	15, 24, 27, 50
Dome of the Rock (Omar Mosque)	8, 9, 13, 14
Du Plat	38
Dragon Wall	59
Eben-ezer	14
Ecole Biblique, St Etienne	12, 13, 48
Eden, Garden of	10, 29, 56
Egypt	55
Ein Kerem	6, 7
Ein (En) Rogel spring	50
El Bireh, Upper Pool	58
El Kas, (The Cup)	11, 12, 14, 15, 24, 30, 46
Elphinstone, Sir Howard	29
Emmaus	8, 31, 39, 40, 55
Euphrates, River	25, 26, 55, 56
Eudocia (Theodosia)	12, 48
Fergusson, James	12
Gebel Uzdom	27
Gennath Gate	42
Giants, Valley of	37, 50
Gibeon	31, 33, 35, 36, 51, 57
Gihon, River	14, 24-26, 41, 55, 56, 58, 59
Glastonbury	56
Golden Gate	42
Gnostics	23
Hemispheres, North and South	27, 28
Herod, the Great, King	15, 42, 45, 46
Herodias, Queen	36
Hezekiah, King of Judah	58, 59
Hippicus, Tower of	22, 41, 42, 44
Hinnom, Valley of	24, 26, 59
Holy of Holies	11, 16, 21, 53
Holy Sepulchre Church	8
Indian Ocean	67
Jaffa Gate	6
Jerome, Saint	15, 31

Jeremiah	7-9, 12-15, 21, 22, 42, 43, 47, 48, 51,
Jerusalem	6-9, 13, 14, 18-23, 30, 31, 34, 35, 39, 48-59
Jordan, Valley	50
Josephus, Flavius	21, 31, 36, 38, 41-44
Kobebeh, al Quebeiba,"Emmaus"	8, 31
Kidron, Cedron	50
Kiriah Jearim	56
Kuryat al Enab	56
Langlais, French Consul	39
Latrun	39, 40
Lazarus	20
Liguria	28
Mamilla Pool	36
Marshallams family	7, 29
Menorah, Temple Lights	55
Meshach	22
Mizpah, Mizpeh	14, 51
Moore, Noel UK Consul	7
Montefiore's Cottages	36
Mount of Olives	6
Mount Moriah	22
Milton	26
Napoleon	39
Nebuchadnezzar, King	42, 43
Nebuzadaradon, Babylonian Chief	43
Neby Samuel (Tomb of Samuel)	14, 51
Nineveh, Assyria	26, 55
Palestine Exploration Fund	31, 35, 51
Persian Gulf	25, 26
Persian Invasion	12
Pison, RIver	26, 27, 55, 56
Potters or Fullers' Field	59
Ramleh, Ramle	39, 51
Rehoboam, King of Judah	18
St Crick, Mlle	31
St Stephen, Stephen's Gate	12, 14, 18, 39, 48, 49

Saul, King	32, 35, 38, 56
Schick, Conrad	12, 51
Septuagint	22, 50, 57-59
Serpents Pool	41
Seychelles	14, 29, 52, 55
Shew Bread Table	13, 47
Shishak, Sheshonk, Pharaoh	18
Skull, Place of (Golgotha)	7-9, 18-24, 30, 32, 36, 39, 43, 51, 55, 56
Sodom	27
Solomon, King	13, 18, 20, 37, 38, 45, 51, 53, 60
Slaughter House, The	7, 39, 47, 54
Sultan of Perak	14
Tabernacle, Sanctuary	10, 11, 20, 31, 35, 45, 54, 55
Tacitus	21
Temple	6-22, 30, 31, 41-45, 53, 55, 60
Theodosia, Empress	12
Titus, "General" of Rome	21, 22, 30, 41-44, 47, 51, 55, 56
Tophet	59
Tombs of the Kings	38
Tower of Funeraries	36
Towers -Mariamne, Psephinus, Phasael	42, 44
Towers of Women	36
Tristram, Canon Henry Baker	27
Tubal	22
Tyropoen Valley	41
Uzzah	50
Victoria, Queen	38
Wilson, Charles	7, 12
Wiseman, Mr (CMS)	7
Wordsworth, Bishop	22, 39
Zion, City of	20, 21, 32, 35, 38, 50, 52, 53, 55

From: The Palestine Exploration Fund Journal April 1885

EDEN AND GOLGOTHA.

By General Charles Gordon, R.E.

I.

Position of Eden.

I HAVE formed a theory with respect to the position of Eden. I believe the Greek of the text respecting the parting of the main river of Eden into four other rivers can be read that four rivers united to form one great river.

In Genesis we have one river Euphrates given us : on it was Babylon. We have the Hiddekel, on which was Nineveh (*vide* Daniel), and which is the Tigris ; these two unite and come down the Persian Gulf. We need to identify the Pison and Gihon. The Pison is the Nile, its meaning is "overflowing," and it flowed into the Red Sea before the Flood ; it is connected with Egypt, which, like Nineveh and Babylon, oppressed Israel. The Blue Nile encompasses Havilah, where there is gold. Havilah was a grandson of Shem, his brothers were Ophir and Sheba, also connected with gold, and with Abyssinia ; they went forth by Mesha (? Mecca), they crossed the sea, for Solomon got his gold from Ophir by sea. Where is the Gihon ? There is the Brook Gihon south of Jerusalem, the Valley of Hinnom, where idolatrous practices went on ; it therefore is also a spot whence Israel was oppressed. On this brook is Jerusalem ; its flow, when it has any, is to the Dead Sea, its ravine is very deep, and could have been the bed of a river before the Flood. There is the difficulty of finding a ravine from the Dead Sea descending to the Gulf of Akabah through Wâdy Arabah, the Valley of Salt. By report, the watershed or flow of the Valley of Salt is towards the Dead Sea, and not towards the Gulf of Akabah. Is there any other ravine from the Dead Sea to the Red Sea by which the Gihon could meet the Nile in that Red Sea ?

Allowing for the moment that the Pison is the Nile, and Gihon is the Brook Gihon, that they flowed into the Red Sea, and through the Gate of the World, Bab el Mandeb, we find by taking off the soundings of the Indian Ocean, that there are two clefts of 1,000 fathoms deep, joining near Socotra, and then going south, gradually deepening till they reach 2,600 fathoms, some 100 or 200 miles west of Seychelles.

Seychelles is granitic, all other isles are volcanic.

Aden, query Eden.

Mussulman tradition places Eden at Ceylon.

I do not go into the question whether or not the Tree of Knowledge is not the *Lodoicea seychellarium*, and the Tree of Life the *Artocarpus incisa*, though for myself I do not doubt it.

I was two years in the neighbourhood of the sources of the Euphrates, Arax, Phasis, &c. ; no flood could connect these rivers ;—floods do not alter the features of a country with respect to high ranges.

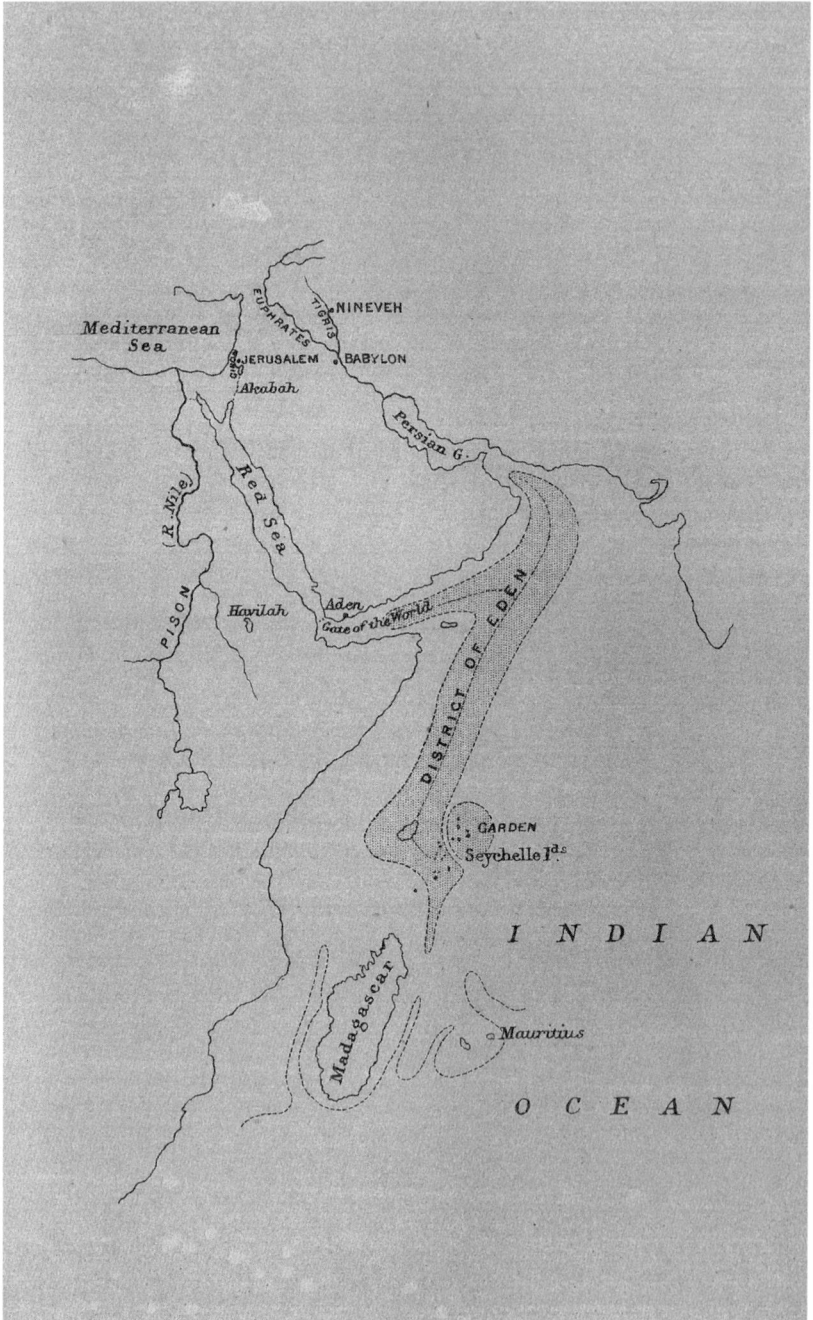

II.

GOLGOTHA.

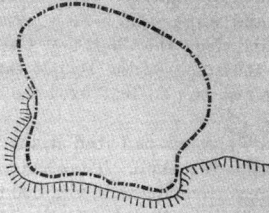

1. I last wrote to you giving the four rivers of Eden, one of which was the Gihon on which Jerusalem was. I do not know if I then mentioned it was the Tyropœon Valley, which conclusion I came to ere I came to Palestine.

2. *Golgotha.* The morning after my arrival at Jerusalem I went to the Skull Hill, and felt convinced that it must be north of the Altar. Leviticus i, 11, says that the victims are to be slain on the side of the Altar northwards (literally to be slain slantwise or askew on the north of the Altar); if a particular direction was given by God about where the types were to be slain, it is a sure deduction that the prototype would be slain in some position as to the Altar: this the Skull Hill fulfils. With reference to the word "askew" or "aslant," we have the verse "all the day long have I stretched out my arms to a rebellious people" (Isa. lxv, 2). Draw a line from the centre of the Sakhra to the centre of the Skull; draw a perpendicular to this line, at centre of skull; a cross on that line will embrace all the city and Mount of Olives, and be askew to the Altar.

The Latin Holy Sepulchre is west of the Altar, and therefore, unless the types are wrong, it should never have been taken as the site.

I pass by the fact of the tradition of Beth hat Selzileh, of the precipice, of the tradition of its being the place Jeremiah wrote the Lamentations (which describes the scenes enacted there nearly 600 years afterwards, "Is it nothing to thee, all ye that pass by" (Lam. i, 12), &c., or the particularly suitable entourage of the place, for these things may be fanciful. I also will not hold to the fact that in the twelfth century St. Stephen's Church was at the Damascus Gate, outside, and St. Stephen was stoned nine months after our Lord's Crucifixion, and that it is unlikely that the Jews would have had two places of execution in nine months.

2. And I will come to the more fanciful view, that the mention of the place of Skull in each four gospels is a call to attention. Wherever a mention of any particular is made frequently, we may rely there is something in it; if the skull is mentioned four times, one naturally looks

for the body, and if you take Warren's or others' contours with the earth or rubbish removed showing the natural state of the land, you cannot help seeing that there is a body, that Schick's conduit is the œsophagus, that the quarries are the chest, and if you are venturesome you will carry out the analogy further. You find also the verse (Ps. xlviii), " Zion, on the sides of the north ;" the word "pleura," same as they pierced His *pleura*, and there came blood and water, God took a *pleuron* from the side of Adam, and made woman. Now the Church of Christ is made up of, or came from, His *pleura*, the stones of the Temple came from the quarries, from chest of figure, and so on ; so that fixed the figure of body to the skull.

3. Then by Josephus's account, as I read it, the Tower Psephinus was on the rocky point opposite the skull. Titus had his headquarters at the slaughter-house, 2 furlongs from the wall, viz., 300 to 400 yards, near the *corner* (note that corner, for it is alluded to in the 400 cubits broken down by Jehoash, king of Israel), and my placing of the walls and reading of Josephus would make his point of attack just where Schick's conduit enters the city east of Damascus Gate, or at the cisterns to east, where I think Agrippa's wall began. Mystically, the Roman Eagle should have gone at the Lamb of Zion by the throat, viz., Schick's conduit. However, I will not continue this, for if you please you can get the papers and plans from my brother. I would do them for you if you wish ; I did them for Chaplin long ago. The camp of the Assyrians is the place where Nebuchadnezzar camped a month *after the fall of the city*, when he came to *burn the Temple ;* it is this day which the Jews keep as the fast, not the day of *taking the city*.

3. Naturally, after discerning *the figure*, the question arose of Mount Zion, and of the boundaries ; by studying the latter with the Septuagint there seemed no reason *by Scripture* to consider Ain Haud the *Enshemesh*. Septuagint has Beth Samos, and near Jebel el Tell is Kh. el Sama. Again, Gihon (being the Tyropœon) is to gush forth, and as the skull is the Altar, it is thence the two rivers, one to the Dead Sea, the other to the Mediterranean, are to come. At last Moses's blessing to Benjamin came in, " he shall rest between His arms," not his shoulders ; so thus I brought the boundary up Gihon to Kh. el Sama.

4. Other reasons came to back this view,—

Nehemiah mentions town of Furnaces.

He also mentions throne of *Governor*.

Josephus mentions women's towers.

The word "furnace" is derived from *fornex*, thence the connection. The tent Cozbi and Zimri went into was a *furnace*. Josiah broke down the high places built by Manasseh near the Gate of *Governor*, which were, no doubt, these same *furnaces*. Herodias lived at Jaffa Gate, and even to this day there are *furnaces* there I should think, for the troops are there.

This led to looking up the history of the Levites, &c., in Judges, of Gibeon, of mouldy bread, Nob, Gibeah of Saul, &c., and the result is as

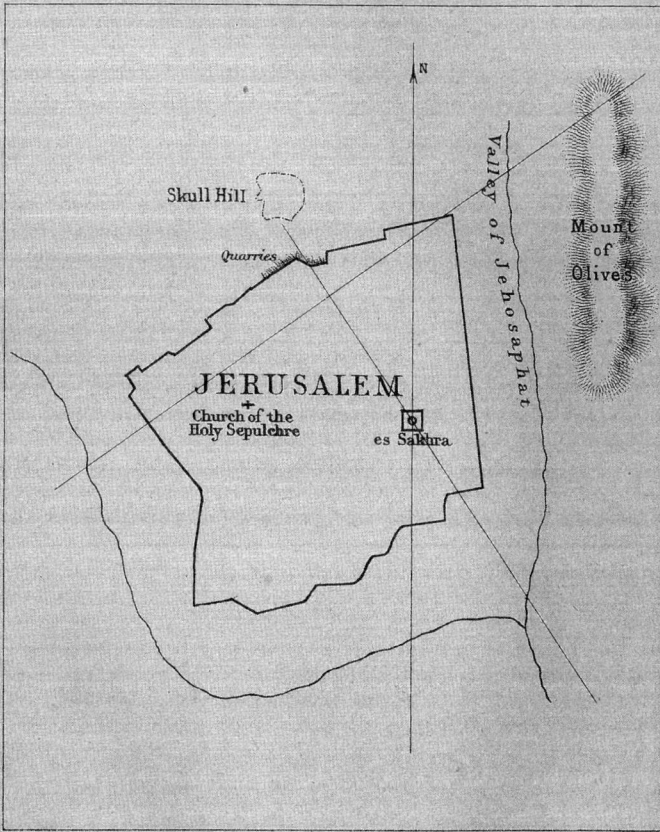

Skull Hill

Quarries

JERUSALEM
+
Church of the
Holy Sepulchre

es Sakhra

Valley of Jehosaphat

Mount
of
Olives

N

E.Weller.

I have just noted, according to my ideas; but it is a matter of perfect indifference to us all, for these sites are in each of us.

During these studies, the potters' field comes up, and also the pool where Abner and Joab met, the field of the treacherous ones, and my idea is that round about the Serpent's Pool is the Tophet, Aceldama, Potters' field ; that down the Valley of Hinnom is the Perez of David.

I will not bore you much longer than to say that, by my ideas,

Kuryet el Eneb is
- Kirjath-jearim
- Ramathaim-Zophim
- Armathaim
- Ramah, one of them
- Place of Saul's anointing
- Arimathæa
- Emmaus

and that Samuel was sacrificing to the Ark when Saul came to him.

Schick has been writing on these subjects for years, and he plaintively says, "but how *am I* possibly to advance other views now ?" In reality, in writing on these sites, no man ought to draw any cheques on his imagination ; he ought to keep to the simple fact, and not prophesy or fill up gaps. If one wrote under cognomen *a*, and altered under cognomen *β* it would be all right ; as it is now, a man under his own name cannot go right about face all at once. The Ark was built at Abu Shusheh by Noah, and floated up to Baris ; only in A.D. 776 was it placed on Ararat, which is "*holy land*." God said, "Go to a mountain I will shew thee," a mountain already consecrated by the resting place of the Ark. Noah offered on the rock his sacrifice. Look at Genesis and you will see (Gen. xi, 1), after the Flood they journeyed *eastward* to Shinar ; you might go eastward from either Ararat or El Judi near Jesereb ebn Omar for ever before you reached Shinar. I will not bore you any longer, except to say that I think there are not many places far apart of interest in the Scripture way, and that these few are—

1. Nazareth and region of Tiberias.
2. Plain of Esdraelon.
3. Shechem.
4. Bethel.
5. Jerusalem.
6. Bethlehem
7. Hebron.
8. Kuryet el Eneb, Philistia.
9. Jericho, Gilgal, Ammon and Moab, Dead Sea, Valley of Arabah.

C. G.

BIRDS EYE VIEW OF JERUSALEM FROM THE SOUTH (COPY OF AN ETCHING)
BY WF WITTS

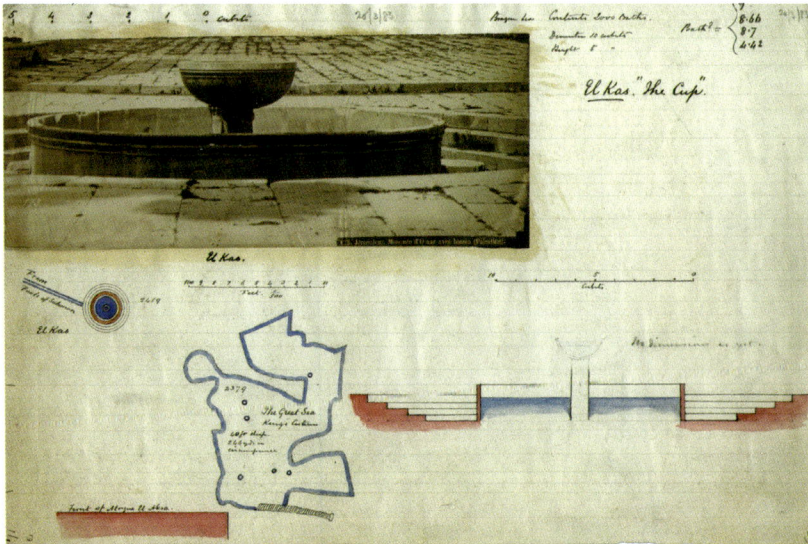

EL KAS AND DIAGRAM OF CISTERNS BENEATH

DIAGRAM OF AREA OF HEROD'S TEMPLE V. SOLOMON'S TEMPLE AREA

BORDERS OF BENJAMIN AND JUDAH

DIAGRAM OF EL KAS – THE CUP AND DOME OF THE ROCK
See The Wailing Place Diagram on next page

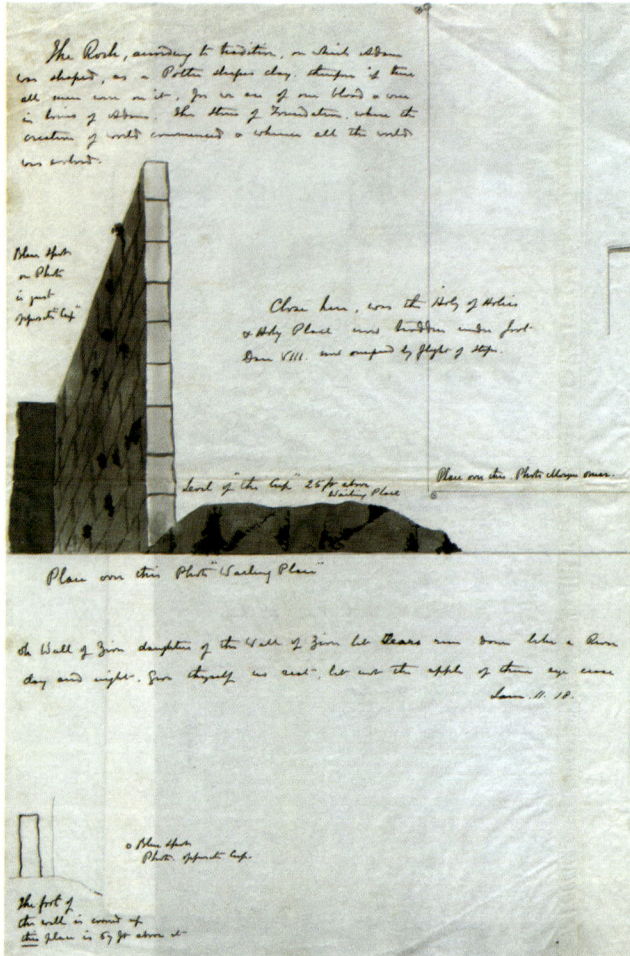

"THE WAILING PLACE" DIAGRAM

The Rock, according to tradition, on which Adam was shaped, as a Potter shapes clay, therefore if true all men were on it, for we are of one blood and were in the loins of Adam. The Stone of Foundation, where the creation of the world commenced and whence all the world was evolved.

Blue spot on photo is just opposite "Cup"

Close here was the Holy of Holies and Holy Place now trodden under foot (Daniel VIII) now accessed by flight of steps.

Place on this Photo of Mosque

Level of "The Cup" 25 feet above Wailing Place

Place over this Photo "Wailing Place"
"Oh Wall of Zion daughters of the Wall of Zion let tears run down like a River day and night. Give thyself rest, let not the apple of thine eye cease." **Lamentations II: 18**

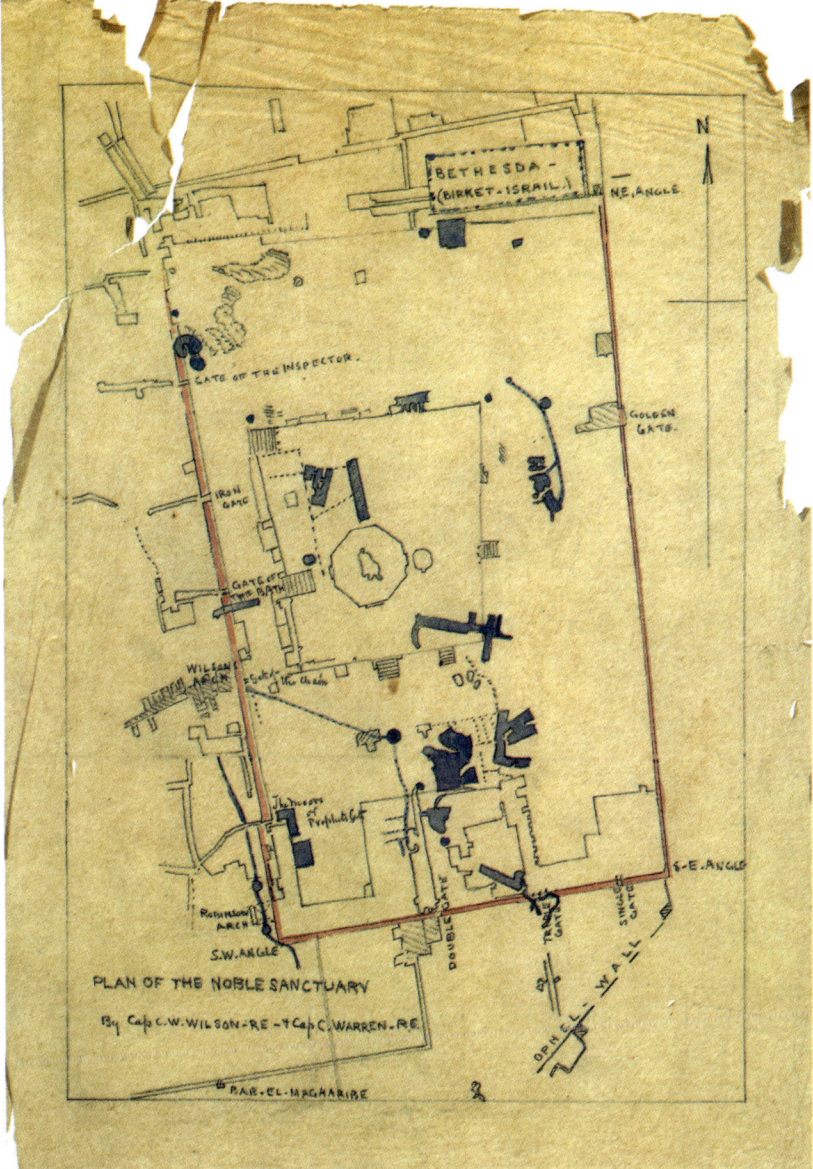

COPY OF MAP OF TEMPLE AREA BY WILSON AND WARREN

THE ROCK – EBEN SHATYA (NAVEL OF THE WORLD)

MAP OF SUPPOSED SOLOMON'S TEMPLE AREA

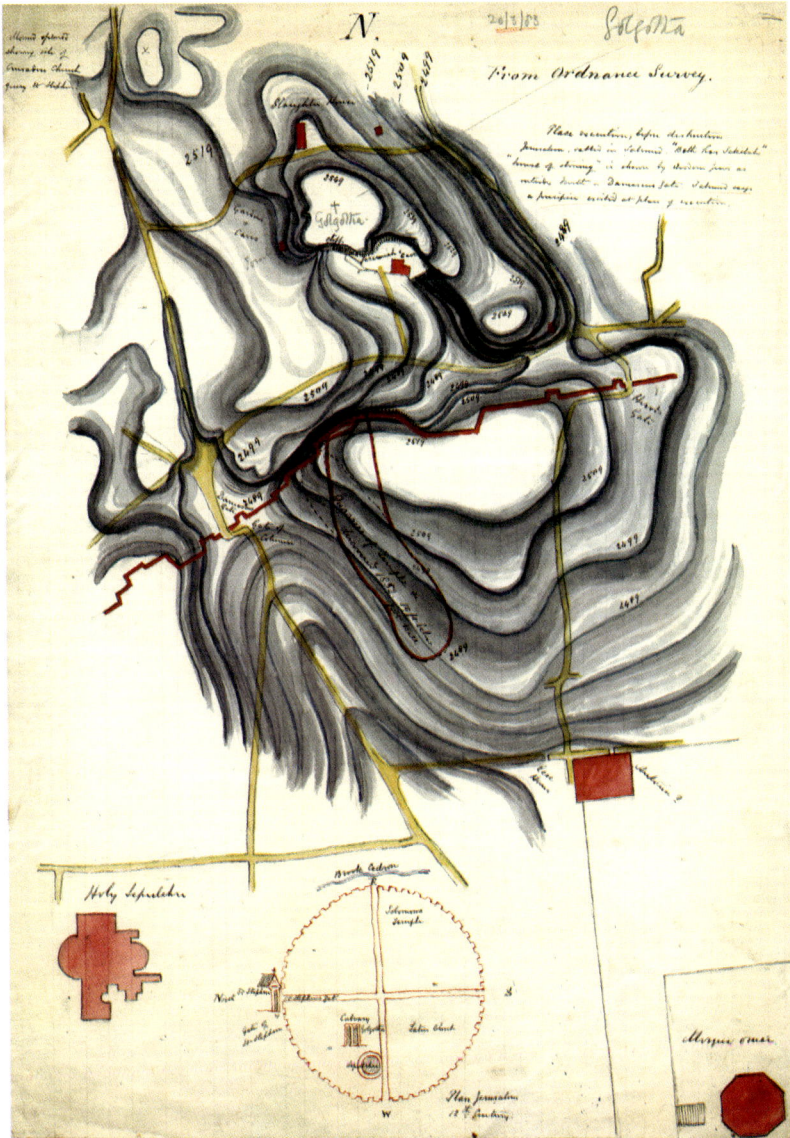

GOLOGOTHA – SURVEY CHART

Left side: Mound opened showing site of Crusaders Church query St. Stephen
Right side: Place execution, before destruction Jerusalem, called in Talmud "Beth has Sekilah" "house of stoning" is shown by modern Jews as outside North of Damascus Gate. Talmud says a precipice existed at place of execution.

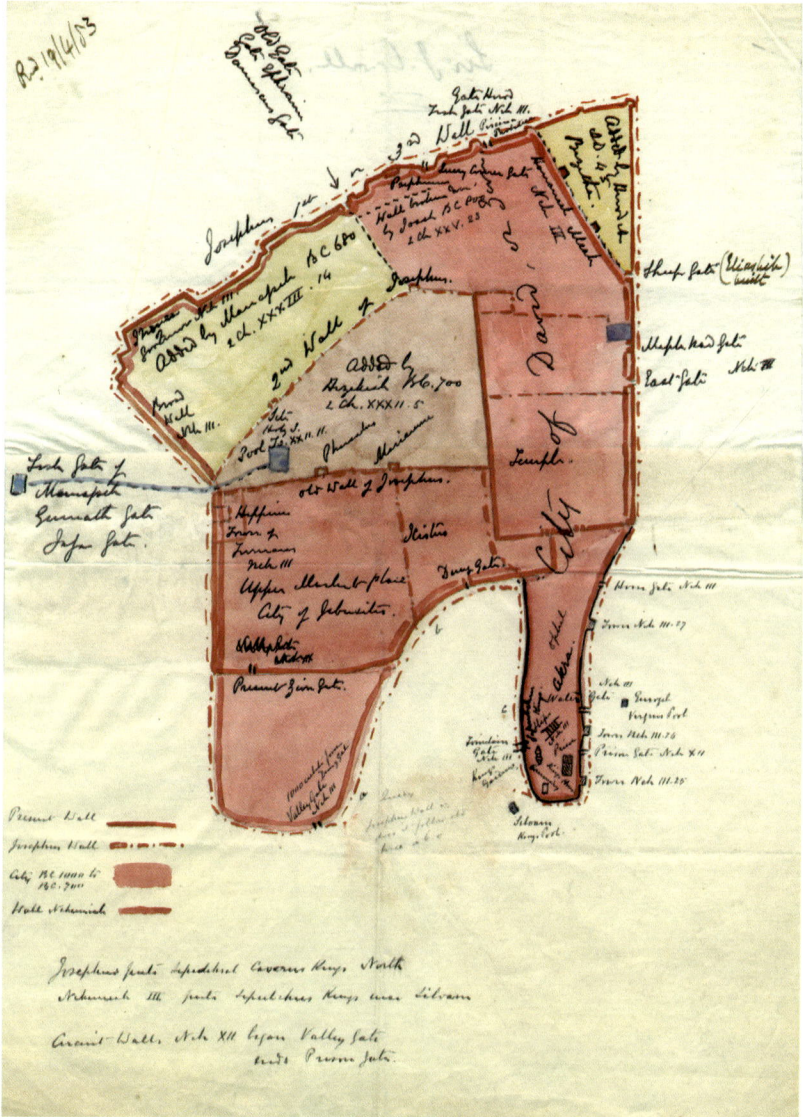

MAP OF CITY LAY OUT IN COLOURED SECTIONS

Note below: Josephus puts sepulchral caverns Kings North
Nehemiah III puts Sepulchres of Kings near Silwan
Ancient Walls Nehemiah XII began Valley Gate, ends Prison Gate

SKETCH OF WALLS OF THE CITY AND ASSAULT POSITIONS
according to Josephus' account of AD 70

THE SLAUGHTER HOUSE
WATERCOLOUR by permission of Ecole Biblique

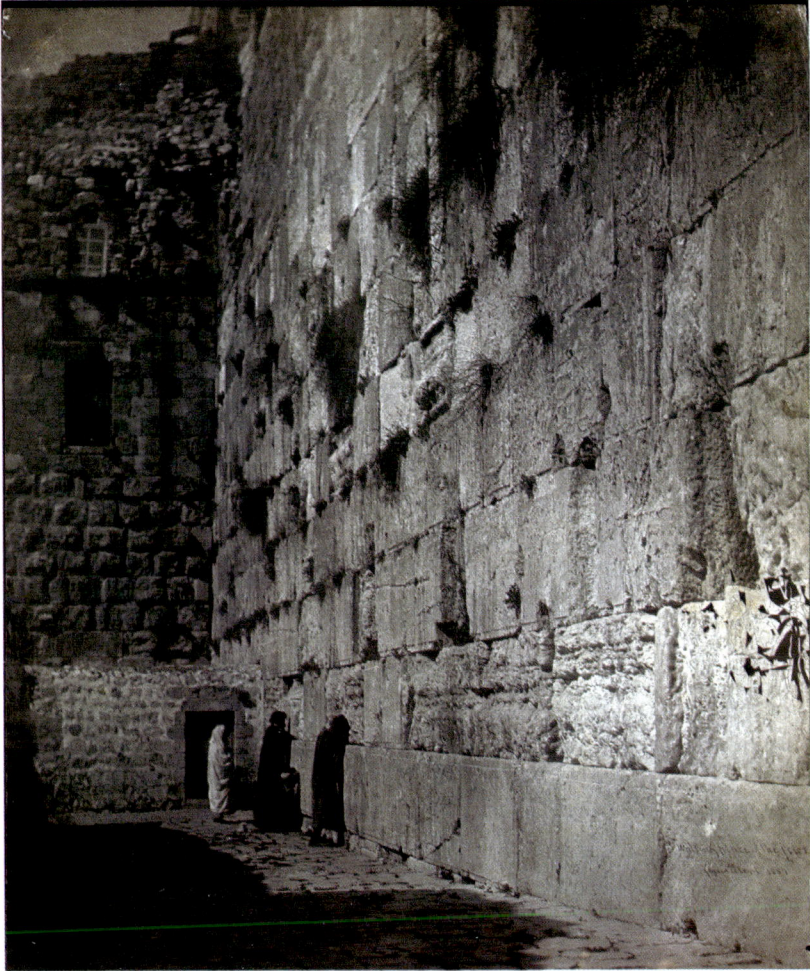

THE WESTERN WALL
C. 1870

THE MOSQUE OF OMAR (Bonfils 170 c.1880)

JEWISH MOURNERS AT WESTERN WALL (Bonfils 154 c. 1880)

THE MOSQUE OF OMAR AND THE CUP (Bonfils 173 c. 1880)

JERUSALEM FROM THE EAST (J Graham c. 1856)

JERUSALEM FROM MOUNT SCOPUS (NORTH-EAST) (J. Graham c. 1856)

JERUSALEM – JEREMIAH'S GROTTO AND "SKULL HILL" (Bonfils 194 c.1880)

THE GARDEN TOMB TODAY

"SKULL HILL" TODAY